Tom Pendergast
& Sara Pendergast,
Editors

Detroit • New York • San Diego • San Francisco • Cleveland • New Haven, Conn. • Waterville, Maine • London • Munich

973
.91
UX
c.4

U•X•L American Decades, 1940–1949

Tom Pendergast and Sara Pendergast, Editors

Project Editors
Diane Sawinski, Julie L. Carnagie, and Christine Slovey

Editorial
Elizabeth Anderson

Permissions
Shalice Shah-Caldwell

Imaging and Multimedia
Dean Dauphinais

Product Design
Pamela A.E. Galbreath

Composition
Evi Seoud

Manufacturing
Rita Wimberley

For permission to use material from this product, submit your request via Web at http://www.gale-edit.com/permissions, or you may download our Permissions Request form and submit your request by fax or mail to:

Permissions Department
The Gale Group, Inc.
27500 Drake Rd.
Farmington Hills, MI 48331-3535
Permissions Hotline:
248-699-8006 or 800-877-4253, ext. 8006
Fax: 248-699-8074 or 800-762-4058

Cover photograph reproduced by permission of the Corbis Corporation.

While every effort has been made to ensure the reliability of the information presented in this publication, The Gale Group, Inc. does not guarantee the accuracy of the data contained herein. The Gale Group, Inc. accepts no payment for listing; and inclusion in the publication of any organization, agency, institution, publication, service, or individual does not imply endorsement of the editors or publisher. Errors brought to the attention of the publisher and verified to the satisfaction of the publisher will be corrected in future editions.

Vol. 1: 0-7876-6455-3
Vol. 2: 0-7876-6456-1
Vol. 3: 0-7876-6457-X
Vol. 4: 0-7876-6458-8
Vol. 5: 0-7876-6459-6
Vol. 6: 0-7876-6460-X
Vol. 7: 0-7876-6461-8
Vol. 8: 0-7876-6462-6
Vol. 9: 0-7876-6463-4
Vol. 10: 0-7876-6464-2

LIBRARY OF CONGRESS CATALOGING-IN-PUBLICATION DATA

U•X•L American decades
 p. cm.
Includes bibliographical references and index.
 Contents: v. 1. 1900-1910—v. 2. 1910-1919—v. 3.1920-1929—v. 4. 1930-1939—v. 5. 1940-1949—v. 6. 1950-1959—v. 7. 1960-1969—v. 8. 1970-1979—v. 9.1980-1989—v. 10. 1990-1999.
 Summary: A ten-volume overview of the twentieth century which explores such topics as the arts, economy, education, government, politics, fashions, health, science, technology, and sports which characterize each decade.
 ISBN 0-7876-6454-5 (set: hardcover: alk. paper)
 1. United States—Civilization—20th century—Juvenile literature. 2. United States—History—20th century—Juvenile literature. [1. United States—Civilization—20th century. 2. United States—History—20th century.] I. UXL (Firm) II. Title: UXL American decades. III. Title: American decades.
E169.1.U88 2003
973.91—dc21
2002010176

Printed in the United States of America
10 9 8 7 6 5 4 3 2

Contents

Reader's Guide

U•X•L American Decades provides a broad overview of the major events and people that helped to shape American society throughout the twentieth century. Each volume in this ten-volume set chronicles a single decade and begins with an introduction to that decade and a timeline of major events in twentieth-century America. Following are eight chapters devoted to these categories of American endeavor:

• Arts and Entertainment

• Business and the Economy

• Education

• Government, Politics, and Law

• Lifestyles and Social Trends

• Medicine and Health

• Science and Technology

• Sports

These chapters are then divided into five sections:

Chronology: A timeline of significant events within the chapter's particular field.

Overview: A summary of the events and people detailed in that chapter.

Headline Makers: Short biographical accounts of key people and their achievements during the decade.

❖ **Topics in the News:** A series of short topical essays describing events and people within the chapter's theme.

✢ **For More Information:** A section that lists books and Web sites directing the student to further information about the events and people covered in the chapter.

OTHER FEATURES

Each volume of *U•X•L American Decades* contains more than eighty black-and-white photographs and illustrations that bring the events and people discussed to life and sidebar boxes that expand on items of high interest to readers. Concluding each volume is a general bibliography of books and Web sites that explore the particular decade in general and a thorough subject index that allows readers to easily locate the events, people, and places discussed throughout that volume of *U•X•L American Decades*.

ACKNOWLEDGMENTS

The editor would like to offer thanks to many people for their help and support during the writing of this book. The series editors, Tom and Sara Pendergast have, as always, been supportive, encouraging, and critical in just the right amounts. James Yardley at <www.ask-a-librarian.org.uk> and Gail Keutzer at the Internet Public Library <www.ipl.org> were extremely helpful with difficult-to-find dates and obscure facts. Thanks to Esme Miskimmin for keeping the editor entertained with tea breaks during long days in the library at the University of Liverpool. And the editor would like to offer thanks to his wife, Siobhan, for putting up with lectures on whatever aspect of American history had been the obsession for the day, and a lot more besides.

COMMENTS AND SUGGESTIONS

We welcome your comments on *U•X•L American Decades* and suggestions for other history topics to consider. Please write: Editors, *U•X•L American Decades,* U•X•L, 27500 Drake Rd., Farmington Hills, MI 48331-3535; call toll-free: 1-800-877-4253; fax: 248-699-8097; or send e-mail via http://www.galegroup.com.

Chronology of the 1940s

1940: **April 3** The Olympic games in Finland are canceled because of the war. The games will not resume until 1948.

1940: **July 8** Trans World Airlines (TWA) begins the first commercial flights using planes with pressurized cabins.

1940: **October 24** The forty-hour workweek begins, two years after it was passed as part of the Fair Labor Standards Act of 1938.

1940: **November 13** Walt Disney's animated film *Fantasia* opens in New York, with Leopold Stokowski conducting the orchestra.

1940: **December** An influenza epidemic begins in California and spreads to Oregon, Washington, New Mexico, Arizona, and Idaho.

1941: *The Maltese Falcon,* directed by John Huston, begins the *film noir* style in Hollywood and makes a star of Humphrey Bogart.

1941: **March 25** The most serious measles epidemic in years breaks out along the East Coast and begins to spread westward across America.

1941: **April** At the Massachusetts Institute of Technology (MIT), the Radiation Laboratory develops a prototype radar machine that can detect aircraft and submarines.

1941: **April 11** For the first time, the Ford Motor Company signs a deal with unions to end a strike involving eighty-five thousand workers.

1941: **May 2** The Federal Communications Commission (FCC) authorizes commercial television broadcasting beginning July 1.

1941: May 5 After successful trials, the antibiotic penicillin is unveiled to the public.

1941: May 16 U.S. Defense Savings Bonds go on sale to raise money for defense efforts.

1941: June 2 Baseball hero Lou Gehrig dies of amyotrophic lateral sclerosis (ALS). The illness has since become known as "Lou Gehrig's Disease."

1941: June 25 President Franklin D. Roosevelt signs Executive Order 8802, banning racial discrimination in the defense industries and setting up the Fair Employment Practices Committee.

1941: July 17 Joe DiMaggio ends his fifty-six-game hitting streak in Cleveland, Ohio.

1941: September A nationwide polio epidemic kills eighty-seven people.

1941: December 7 The Japanese sneak attack on Pearl Harbor, Hawaii, leads President Roosevelt to declare war.

1941: December 22 A new military draft act requires all males aged eighteen to sixty-five to register for military service. Those between twenty and forty-four had to be prepared to be called up for active duty.

1942: Napalm is developed for use in U.S. Army flame throwers.

1942: *Casablanca,* one of the most successful movies of all time, opens.

1942: January The College Entrance Examination Board overhauls its testing methods. Instead of the traditional essay test, students begin taking tests measuring reading ability, problem-solving skills, and general knowledge.

1942: January 1 The Declaration of the United Nations is signed, with the United States as one of twenty-six signatories.

1942: February 19 In Executive Order 9066, President Roosevelt orders the removal of all Japanese Americans to internment camps for the rest of the war.

1942: June President Roosevelt approves the Manhattan Project, a secret research program that will eventually build and explode the first atomic bomb. The project is funded with $400 million of federal money.

1943: For the first time, radar is used to guide a plane to a landing.

1943: The antibiotic streptomycin is discovered.

1943: **June 10** The Current Tax Payment Act takes effect. For the first time, Americans have taxes deducted from their paychecks.

1943: **June 20** When African Americans are brought into war industries, race riots break out in Detroit, Michigan. In two days, thirty-five people are killed and five hundred are wounded, most of them black.

1943: **November** President Roosevelt proposes the Vocational Rehabilitation Act, later to become the GI Bill of Rights, the goal of which is to provide education for soldiers returning from military service.

1944: **April 3** In *Smith* v. *Allwright,* the U.S. Supreme Court rules that blacks cannot be denied the right to vote in the Texas Democratic primary.

1944: **July** At the Bretton Woods Conference, held in New Hampshire, international diplomats set up the World Bank, International Monetary Fund (IMF), and the General Agreement on Tariffs and Trade (GATT).

1944: **December 15** Band leader Glenn Miller dies in a plane crash on a trip from London, England, to Paris, France.

1945: **February** Penicillin that can be taken orally is introduced.

1945: **May 23** Typhus patients are treated successfully with streptomycin for the first time.

1945: **November 1–16** The United Nations Educational, Scientific, and Cultural Organization (UNESCO) is founded.

1945: **December 16** A new sulfa drug, metachloride, proves successful in treating malaria.

1946: The segregation of blacks and whites on interstate buses is declared unconstitutional.

1946: **April 14** The movie *So Goes My Love* premiers on a PanAm Clipper flight from New York to Ireland. It is the first film to be screened on a scheduled airline flight.

1946: **July 1** *Oklahoma!* reaches its 1,405th performance on Broadway, the record for a musical.

1946: **August** Public Law 584, known as the Fulbright Act, is passed by Congress. The act provides assistance for students and academics to travel around the world to study in order to encourage cultural understanding.

1946: **August 1** The U.S. Atomic Energy Commission (AEC) begins its job of monitoring and controlling nuclear power.

1947: Using a type of carbon known as carbon-14, chemist Willard Libby develops his radiocarbon-dating method. This is the technique used to establish the age of archaeological finds, among other things.

1947: The cold war puts an end to many of UNESCOs educational programs in developing countries.

1947: **April 10** Jackie Robinson becomes the first black player in major league baseball in the twentieth century after he signs with the Brooklyn Dodgers. In September, he is named rookie of the year by the *Sporting News.*

1947: **September 29** The play *Annie Get Your Gun* is banned in Memphis, Tennessee, because its cast is multiracial.

1947: **September 30** The first televised World Series begins. It is sponsored by Gillette Safety Razor and Ford Motor Company, each of whom pay $65,000 for the privilege. The New York Yankees go on to win their eleventh World Series, beating the Brooklyn Dodgers four games to three.

1947: **October** Separate education for blacks and whites is condemned by the President's Committee on Civil Rights.

1947: **October 13** The anticommunist House Un-American Activities Committee (HUAC) begins cross-examining the Hollywood Ten (a group of movie actors, writers, and production artists). They refuse to testify.

1947: **November 8** Under the Marshall Plan, the U.S. government proposes to give European countries $17 billion to help reconstruct their economies after World War II.

1948: New Jersey desegregates its public schools. From now on, black and white students in New Jersey will study together.

1948: **March 8** In *McCollum* v. *Board of Education,* the U.S. Supreme Court outlaws religious education or activity in public schools.

1948: **June 21** The U.S. Supreme Court rules that unions may not be prevented from publishing political opinions.

1948: **November 4** American poet T. S. Eliot is awarded the Nobel Prize for literature.

1949: The House Un-American Activities Commission (HUAC) requires that lists of books used in courses be submitted for inspection. The Commission is looking for Communist Party propaganda.

1949: **February 27** The American Cancer Society and the National Cancer Institute issue a report linking smoking with lung cancer.

1949: **March 2** The U.S. Air Force Superfortress B-50, known as *Lucky Lady,* completes the first nonstop flight around the world.

1949: **March 7** American League batting champion Ted Williams becomes the highest-paid baseball player ever when he signs with the Boston Red Sox for $100,000 per year.

1949: **April 4** The North Atlantic Treaty Organization (NATO) is founded as a defense pact among the Western Allies.

1949: **August 3** The National Basketball Association (NBA) is formed when the Basketball Association of America and the National Basketball League merge.

1949: **November 19** Jackie Robinson becomes the first black player to be named the National League's Most Valuable Player by the Baseball Writers' Association.

The 1940s: An Overview

Events in the 1940s helped to shape the politics, economics, and culture of the following half century. The first half of the decade was dominated by World War II (1939–45). The war swept away the economic structures that led to the Great Depression (1930–39) and forced rapid developments in medicine, science, and technology. Women and minority groups found they were more involved in industry and government than ever before. All areas of American life were affected by the war. Sports and movie stars served in the military alongside ordinary Americans. Artists, writers, and filmmakers responded first to World War II, and then, after 1945, to the tensions of the cold war. For many Americans the end of the war marked the beginning of a new way of life. They had more money than before, they lived in their own houses in new suburbs, and drove powerful, streamlined automobiles. For most Americans the final years of the decade were a period of optimism, confidence, and hope for the future.

The United States had been a reluctant participant in World War II. The country joined in actual combat only after the Japanese attack on Pearl Harbor, Hawaii, on December 7, 1941. Before that the United States had spent the previous two years supplying arms and war supplies to the Allied nations, including Great Britain and France. Increased spending on military factories boosted the American economy. After 1945, with its factories still intact, the United States became the dominant world economic power. Americans benefitted from cheaper consumer goods and higher salaries. Medicine offered cures for killer diseases such as tuberculosis, while air travel, television, and dramatic sports seasons all gave grounds for optimism. At first even the atomic bomb seemed like a reason to feel more secure than before.

The politics of the postwar world were fundamentally different from what went before. As one of the few countries undamaged by enemy bombing, the United States soon took its place as the leading power among the Western democratic nations. Before 1940, the British Empire had been the major trading and diplomatic power. Now, after 1945, the United States government had to bring order to the chaos of Europe and East Asia. Through the Marshall Plan, the North Atlantic Treaty Organization (NATO), and the World Bank, the administration of President Harry S Truman worked with other governments to rebuild shattered markets and bring political stability. In many ways the late 1940s saw unprecedented cooperation between nations. But it also saw the expansion of the Soviet Union, and the beginning of a military stalemate between East and West that would last until the late 1980s. It was a stalemate overshadowed by a new and deadly weapon, the atomic bomb.

Arts and Entertainment

1940: Charlie Chaplin's film *The Great Dictator* attacks the European dictatorships responsible for World War II (1939–45).

1940: Jazz singer Billie Holiday challenges audiences with her antilynching protest song, "Strange Fruit."

1940: **November 13** Walt Disney's animated film *Fantasia* opens in New York, with Leopold Stokowski conducting the orchestra.

1940: **December 21** Writer F. Scott Fitzgerald dies in Hollywood at the age of forty-four.

1941: *The Maltese Falcon,* directed by John Huston, begins the *film noir* style in Hollywood and makes a star of Humphrey Bogart.

1941: **January 27** Publisher William Randolph Hearst puts his art collection, including around ten thousand items, on private display in New York.

1941: **May 2** The Federal Communications Commission (FCC) authorizes commercial television broadcasting beginning July 1.

1942: *Casablanca,* one of the most successful movies of all time, opens. The script had arrived at Warner Bros. studio the day after the Pearl Harbor attack, and the movie matched the determined mood of the nation.

1942: **February 8** Artist Mark Rothko holds his first solo exhibit at the Artists' Gallery in New York City.

1942: **April 16** The New York Drama Critics' Circle decides there is no play good enough to receive the 1941–42 best play award.

1942: **August 1** The American Federation of Musicians begins a strike against the recording industry. The strike lasts for a whole year.

1943: **September 19** Decca Records becomes the only record label able to produce albums after it strikes a deal with the American Federation of Musicians.

1943: **December 9** Singer Frank Sinatra is declared "4-F," or unfit to fight in the war, because of a punctured eardrum. His career suffers because of his lack of combat duty.

1944: **February 1** Dutch abstract artist Piet Mondrian dies in New York, aged seventy-two.

1944: **August 7** The Justice Department orders motion picture producers to end theater ownership and allow competition in film distribution.

1944: **December 15** Band leader Glenn Miller dies in a plane crash on a trip from London to Paris.

1945: **March 28** British poet W. H. Auden wins the American Academy of Arts and Letters poetry prize.

1945: **May 5** American poet Ezra Pound is arrested in Genoa, Italy, by American armed forces because he allegedly made treasonous radio broadcasts during the war.

1946: **March 13** Twelve poems by Ezra Pound are included in the new edition of *An Anthology of Famous English and American Poetry*. It had been thought none would be included because of his alleged treason.

1946: **April 14** The movie *So Goes My Love* is premiered on a PanAm Clipper flight from New York to Ireland. It is the first film to be screened on a scheduled airline flight.

1946: **July 1** *Oklahoma!* reaches its 1,405th performance on Broadway, the record for a musical.

1947: **January 24** The Metropolitan Museum of Art displays sixty British masterpieces on loan from King George VI.

1947: **September 29** The play *Annie Get Your Gun* is banned in Memphis, Tennessee, because its cast is multiracial.

1947: **October 13** The House Un-American Activities Committee (HUAC) begins cross-examining the Hollywood Ten (a group of movie actors, writers, and production artists). They refuse to testify.

1947: **December 3** The Screen Directors' Guild bans members of the Communist Party from holding office in their organization.

1948: **March 27** Billie Holiday performs at Carnegie Hall in New York, after spending almost a year in prison for possession of narcotics.

1948: **October 6** The Museum of Modern Art in New York City purchases its first painting by Willem de Kooning, titled *Painting*.

1948: **October 30** Under pressure from the courts, RKO Studios agrees to separate its film production and distribution from its theater network.

1948: **November 4** American poet T. S. Eliot is awarded the Nobel Prize for literature.

1948: **November 29** The Metropolitan Opera season opens with Verdi's *Otello*. For the first time, a Met production appears on television.

1949: **February 19** Ezra Pound wins the Bollingen poetry prize. His win upsets many people because he had supported America's opponents during the war. Later in the year, the Library of Congress abolishes its prizes for art, music, and literature because of Pound's win.

1949: **May 23** The Hollywood Ten file suit against Hollywood producers. They had lost their jobs for refusing to testify before the House Un-American Activities Committee (HUAC).

Overview

The 1940s began with the end of one crisis and the start of another. American artists and writers in the 1930s had worked hard to understand and expose the problems caused by unemployment, poverty, and industrial life in the Great Depression (1930–39). Realistic artworks were popular in the 1930s, and many artists continued to create them into the 1940s. But as American society changed with the end of the Depression and the coming of World War II (1939–45), the arts began to reflect new concerns. As Americans grew richer, there was less interest in art that campaigned against poverty. Artists began to look away from society and into themselves for inspiration. In Hollywood, many filmmakers abandoned light entertainment to create films that took a dark view of human nature. Painters turned to abstract images, while writers began to experiment with new forms of poetry and prose.

The 1940s were dominated by war. Many artists and writers had been worried about the rise of fascism (a form of government controlled by a dictator and known for oppression of opposing viewpoints) for years. Some even fought against fascists in the Spanish civil war during the 1930s. But the Japanese bombing of the American port of Pearl Harbor in Hawaii on December 7, 1941, forced the whole nation to take notice of international affairs. From then on, campaigns to help the poor lost support as the nation focused on defeating fascism in Europe and Asia during World War II. Once the war was won, America prospered. Instead of looking outward to society, American artists looked inward to the self.

The ideas behind modernism (a self-conscious break with the past and a search for new forms of expression) emerged in Europe in the 1910s, 1920s, and 1930s, finally taking hold in America in the early 1940s. Modernist art moved away from realism and looked for new forms of expression. American painters began exploring cubism, a style of painting in which images are made up of jumbled, square-edged shapes. Surrealism also had its followers; this style of art shows everyday objects in unusual settings. By the end of the decade, American art was dominated by abstract expressionism. Abstract expressionist painters tried to express their thoughts and feelings through abstract images.

Like painting, music also turned toward individual expression in the 1940s. In bebop, jazz musicians experimented with rhythm, musical forms, and sounds. The long solos of saxophonist Charlie Parker and trumpeter Miles Davis marked a dramatic shift of focus to the individual musician. A similar change was going on in literature. Writers moved away from political themes to focus on the self. Many were influenced by the French philosophy called existentialism. Existentialists argued that individuals are defined by the decisions they make. This was an optimistic view, in the sense that individuals were free to do as they pleased. But it was also frightening. In an existential world, individuals also have to take the consequences for what they do.

Hollywood dealt with World War II in several ways. Many stars enlisted in the armed forces, while others traveled around the battlefields entertaining the troops. Back at home, war movies showed American soldiers beating an evil enemy. After the war ended, Hollywood was less confident. The U.S. Justice Department challenged the movie studios' monopoly on movie distribution. Anticommunists in government attacked the film industry as subversive and dangerous. Television began to spread, bringing competition for the first time. Filmmakers in Hollywood also began to experiment. A style of films known as *film noir* showed a dark, violent underside to American life. By the end of the decade, the shadowy *noir* look dominated the shrinking film industry.

The 1940s were disappointing years for American drama. Only two major voices, playwrights Tennessee Williams and Arthur Miller, emerged during the decade. Drama did not join in the modernist experiment, remaining realistic. But while 1930s theater was often political and forward-looking, 1940s American drama was pessimistic about the future of American society.

Unlike drama, other kinds of American writing developed a great deal during the 1940s. Writers from the so-called "lost generation," such as Ernest Hemingway and F. Scott Fitzgerald, either had died or fallen silent. Works by William Faulkner, an important voice in the 1930s, went out of print in the 1940s. Realist authors such as John Dos Passos kept writing, but a new generation was emerging. Saul Bellow would go on to be one of the most important writers of the century. In 1948, Norman Mailer wrote *The Naked and the Dead,* which is possibly the finest novel to come out of any war. Truman Capote and Gore Vidal also began their writing careers during the decade. In the 1940s, black writers such as Richard Wright also began to influence mainstream literature.

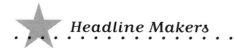

Humphrey Bogart (1899–1957) Born in New York City, Humphrey Bogart began acting on the stage in the 1920s. He signed with Warner Brothers in 1930 and made a series of gangster movies. Bogart became a big star in 1941, when he starred in *The Maltese Falcon,* developing the tough, cynical style that made him a legend. He went on to appear in some of the most important films of the 1940s, including *Casablanca* (1942) and *To Have and Have Not* (1944). Bogart also was a strong supporter of the Hollywood Ten. *Photo reproduced by permission of the Kobal Collection.*

Martha Graham (1895–1991) Martha Graham was the most influential person in dance during the twentieth century. She was comfortable with a wide range of styles and influences, from Native American to experimental modern. She even choreographed dance steps to part of the Declaration of Independence. In the 1940s, she produced some of her finest work, including *Appalachian Spring* (1944) and *Night Journey* (1946). She danced in her last public performance in 1969, at the age of seventy-four. *Photo reproduced by permission of AP/Wide World Photos.*

Lillian Hellman (1906–1984) Playwright Lillian Hellman is regarded as one of the major American playwrights of the twentieth century. Her plays were dominated with social-justice themes that provoked controversy. She wrote many screen plays and books, and she contributed to numerous anthologies and magazines. In 1952, Hellman was called to appear before the House Un-American Activities Committee. She was blacklisted and forced to sell some of her holdings to meet financial obligations. Hellman received many awards during her life, including the New York Drama Critics Circle Award and Academy Award nominations for the screenplays *The Little Foxes* and *The North Star.* *Photo reproduced by permission of AP/Wide World Photos.*

Billie Holiday (1915–1959) At the age of twelve, jazz singer Billie Holiday was working as a prostitute in Baltimore, Maryland. In the late 1920s, she moved with her mother to New York City and began singing in clubs. She sang with the famous big bands of the era, but she went solo in 1938. By the early 1940s, critics recognized Holiday as one of the greatest jazz singers of all time, at the peak of her powers. But Holiday also was addicted to alcohol and heroin. Her career was effectively over by 1950. She died under house arrest for possession of narcotics. *Photo reproduced by permission of AP/Wide World Photos.*

Carson McCullers (1917–1967) At the age of seventeen, after traveling from Columbus, Georgia, to New York City, Carson McCullers lost a large sum of money on the New York subway. This money had been earmarked to pay her fees at the Juilliard School of Music. She then had to concentrate on taking writing classes at Columbia University. Just six years later, she became a famous writer, with three world-class novels to her name. After winning the New York Drama Critics' Circle Award of 1948–49 for *The Member of the Wedding,* her career came to a painful end. Her husband committed suicide, a series of projects failed, and her health faltered. Yet in her short career, McCullers produced some of the finest writing ever to come out of the South. *Photo reproduced by permission of AP/Wide World Photos.*

Frank Sinatra (1915–1998) Frank Sinatra became famous after 1940, but he had spent many years working in clubs before his solo career took off. He enjoyed a string of hit records and toured the world. But in 1947, Sinatra's political views threatened to ruin his career. He had associated with known Communists and his liberal views were unpopular. A switch to acting saved Sinatra from obscurity in the 1950s, and his singing career recovered. He is widely admired as one of the finest popular singers of the twentieth century. *Photo reproduced by permission of the Kobal Collection.*

Orson Welles (1915–1985) Orson Welles is one of the most revered figures of the 1940s in Hollywood. Yet after the 1940s, Hollywood practically ignored him. As a sixteen-year-old, unknown actor, Welles won a part in a play at the Gate Theatre in Dublin, Ireland. In 1938, he narrated the *War of the Worlds* radio broadcast about a false invasion of Earth by aliens, which brought panic to New York streets. But it is for his masterpiece, *Citizen Kane* (1941), that Welles is best remembered. The movie is regularly voted the best of all time for its huge scope and dramatic visuals. Welles appeared in several other movies, wrote two novels, and worked in theater and television for his entire life. *Photo reproduced by permission of the Kobal Collection.*

Richard Wright (1908–1960) In the 1930s, Richard Wright was linked with the Communist Party and with the Federal Writers' Project. His second novel, *Native Son* (1940), is full of anger and frustration. Its main character, Bigger Thomas, finds himself freed of his racial hatred after he murders a white girl. The novel won Wright respect as a writer, but it also made him enemies. In 1947, under pressure in America because of his left-wing politics and finding France a more liberal place, Wright moved to Paris. He lived there until his death. *Photo reproduced by permission of the Fisk University Library.*

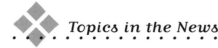

Topics in the News

❖ AMERICA DISCOVERS ITS OWN ART FORM

A small group of American artists had been experimenting with abstract art in New York in the 1930s. They were funded by the Federal Arts Project (FAP), one of many government programs that made up the New Deal. Federal funding removed financial pressures from artists and allowed them to try new things. But a more important influence on American art came from Europe. As the war began in 1939, many artists fled to the United States from Germany, France, and other countries. Dutch painter Piet Mondrian (1872–1944), who arrived in 1940, was among the most influential. Other European expatriates included French painter Marc Chagall (1887–1985), who designed murals for the Metropolitan Opera House in New York. German Max Ernst (1891–1976) and Spaniard Salvador Dali (1904–1989) also spent time in New York. Mondrian, who already was famous when he arrived in America, gave his first (and only) solo exhibition in New York in January 1942. The Europeans encouraged American artists to move away from realistic paintings and create images based on dreams and feelings instead.

In 1939, the Museum of Non-Objective Painting opened in New York City. By that time, there were twenty-one hundred artists in New York, all receiving pay from FAP run by the Works Progress Administration (WPA). Another thousand hopefuls were on the waiting list. Among those working on the FAP were such notables as Willem de Kooning (1904–1997), Lee Krasner (1908–1984), and Mark Rothko (1903–1970). Years later, Jackson Pollock (1912–1956) said he was grateful to the WPA for "keeping me alive during the thirties."

The key year in the development of American art of the decade was 1942. Artists such as Mondrian and Rothko held solo exhibits early in the year. At a gallery called McMillen Inc., in New York, American and European artists exhibited together. And in the fall of 1942, Peggy Guggenheim (1898–1979) opened the Art of This Century Gallery, showing contemporary American art alongside masterpieces of the early twentieth century. The gallery became the center of what is known as the New York School. William Baziotes (1912–1963), Pollock, and others exhibited there. Most importantly, it introduced the world to abstract expressionism, the style of painting that defined American art in the twentieth century.

The term "abstract expressionism" was first used by art critic Robert Coates (1897–1973) in a *New Yorker* article in March 1946. It has come to refer to a single group of artists working in New York in the 1940s. But in fact, the abstract expressionists can be divided into three main groups: the "action" painters, the "color field" painters, and other painters not so easily defined, such as Philip Guston (1913–1980) and Adolph Gottlieb (1903–1974).

The best-known action painters are Jackson Pollock and Willem de Kooning. They worked on huge canvases that usually were laid out on the floor. They applied paint by pouring and dripping, or by using their own bodies or objects such as bicycles to spread it around. The aim was to be as close to the painting as possible. Above all, action paintings record the action as it takes place. The color field painters were led by Mark Rothko (1903–1970), Adolph "Ad" Reinhardt (1913–1967), and Barnett Newman (1905–1970). Their paintings involved huge flat areas or "fields" of a single color. Where these fields of color meet they often bleed together. Rothko thought realistic painting could not express human emotion after World War II. His fields of intense color overwhelm the viewer with their presence and beauty.

Abstract artist Jackson Pollock's painting Number 23, *1948.* **Reproduced by permission of Art Resource.**

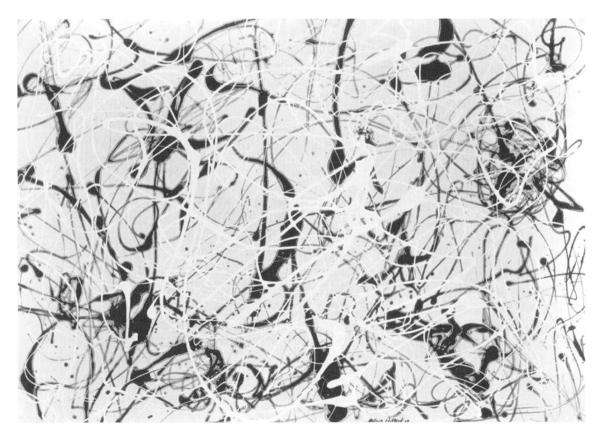

Art and African Americans

Until the 1940s, African Americans made very little impact on the white art world. Jacob Lawrence (1917–2000) was one of the first black artists to gain mainstream attention. His series, *The Migration of the Negro* (1940–41), contains sixty paintings telling the story of black Americans. Lawrence taught at Black Mountain College in North Carolina. By the end of the decade, he was acclaimed as one of the most important American artists of the period. Black artists were given another boost by the book *Modern Negro Art* (1943). In this work, James A. Porter (1905–1970) catalogued the work of black artists up to that point. Porter rescued many neglected African American artists from obscurity.

Abstract expressionist painting is generally not realistic; rather, it tries to express thoughts, feelings, myths, and dreams. Abstract expressionists began to split into even smaller groups as the decade went on. But all the painters involved kept their interest in expressing emotions through painting. In abstract expressionism, America finally had a form of art it could call its own.

❖ A GOLDEN AGE FOR COMIC BOOKS

The comic book was invented in the United States around 1933. By 1940, it had developed into a sophisticated and highly popular form of literature. That year, more than 150 titles were in print covering categories from crime, fantasy, romance, and horror to Westerns and war. But two characters dominated comic book sales in the 1940s. Superman, created by Jerry Siegel (1914–1996) and Joe Shuster (1914–1992), had appeared in 1938. Batman, created by Bob Kane (1915–1998), had first emerged from the Batcave in 1939. By 1940, both Superman and Batman comics were bestsellers. Hoping to ride on their success, National Periodical Publications introduced many other caped and costumed heroes, including the Flash, Hawkman, and the Green Lantern. Captain Marvel first appeared in *Whizz Comics* in 1940, and Captain America in 1941. Like Captain Marvel, Plastic Man added a humorous edge to an otherwise mostly serious, patriotic group of characters.

After World War II ended, patriotic fervor began to die away. Western and romance stories then became more popular than superhero comics.

After runaway success in the 1930s, pulp magazines such as *Black Mask* began to lose their readership in the 1940s. One reason for this was the rise of the paperback book. Allen Lane (1902–1970) introduced Penguin paperbacks in Britain in 1936. Penguin inspired Robert Fair de Graff (1895–1981) to found Pocket Books in the United States in 1939. Other publishers moved into the market. Paperbacks soon became the most popular form of book publishing. In 1947, crime writer Mickey Spillane (1918–) published his first novel, *I, The Jury,* in hardcover. It sold reasonably well—for a hardback. The following year, Signet released a paperback edition. It had sold an amazing two million copies by the end of the decade.

Crime stories also became popular. The series *Crime Does Not Pay* began in 1942. But crime comics certainly did pay. By 1945, the crime comic had become one of the top-selling comics in America. Pictures of scantily dressed women meant that crime comics were deemed unsuitable for children. As concern about the content of crime comics grew, they were toned down. By the 1950s, crime-comic publishers had become very careful about what appeared in their magazines.

Because of the large number of titles on sale, the 1940s is known as the golden age of comic books. Yet original examples are hard to find. They were considered throwaway items, and were often discarded after they had been read. Some were destroyed in protests about their content. Many others were pulped (recycled) during wartime paper shortages. In the twentieth century, there has arisen a thriving collectors' market for comic books from the 1940s.

❖ AMERICAN FICTION REACTS TO THE REAL WORLD

The 1940s was a decade of change in American literature. During the 1930s, many American writers described the terrible suffering caused by the Great Depression. Writers such as Theodore Dreiser (1871–1945) and Sinclair Lewis (1885–1951) had built careers writing fiction that documented the American experience. But 1939 marked the end of a period of realism in American fiction. The group of writers known as the "lost generation" was also slipping out of favor. F. Scott Fitzgerald

(1896–1940) died as the 1940s began. Ernest Hemingway (1899–1961) published *For Whom the Bell Tolls* in 1940, then fell silent for several years. Even William Faulkner (1897–1962), who won the 1949 Nobel Prize in literature (awarded in 1950), wrote mostly screenplays in the 1940s. An era in American fiction was ending, and a new one was just beginning.

The alternative to realism was modernism. Modernist writers saw no need to describe the lives of working people. They veered away from commentating directly on society. In the hands of Europeans in the 1920s and earlier, the novel had begun to focus on the unique viewpoint of a single individual. Simple story lines and narratives were abandoned, and inventive new ways were found to describe characters. Yet among American writers, only Faulkner and John Dos Passos (1896–1970) had experimented with modernist techniques before the 1940s. American writers were slow to respond to the trend in the new fiction.

American journalist and novelist Norman Mailer has won many literary awards, including two Pulitzer Prizes. Reproduced by permission of the Estate of Carl Van Vechten.

Then, in 1944, Saul Bellow (1915–) published *Dangling Man,* a novel about an individual's response to the modern world. Other modernist writers, including Truman Capote (1924–1984) and Chester Himes (1909–1984), followed Bellow. But what would become a major movement in American fiction was only just beginning. In the 1940s realist writers were still producing important work. Robert Penn Warren (1905–1989) won the Pulitzer Prize for *All the King's Men* in 1946. Women writers Carson McCullers (1917–1967) and Eudora Welty (1909–2001) both were influential figures in regionalist fiction (fiction based in a particular location), describing life in the South.

There were other influences on American fiction besides modernism in the 1940s. Many young writers experienced combat in World War II (1939–45), and it was inevitable that novels about the war would start to appear. The two most influential combat novelists were John Hawkes (1925–1998) and Norman Mailer (1923–). Hawkes's novel *The Cannibal* (1949) examined the culture of war and its aftermath. Mailer's *The Naked and the Dead* (1948) established him as one of the major writers of postwar America.

While the novel in general was going through a period of change, black writers were also starting to be noticed by the general reading public. The publication of *Native Son* in 1940 was a turning point for black fiction. The novel made its author, Richard Wright (1908–1960), into a prominent literary figure. Many commentators disagreed with Wright's vision of blacks in America, but because of *Native Son,* white America suddenly took notice of black writers. Zora Neale Hurston (1891– 1960) and Chester Himes (1909–1984) also became well known during the 1940s, while James Baldwin (1924–1987) was just beginning his career as the decade ended.

❖ HOLLYWOOD GOES TO WAR

After a decade of lavish musicals, screwball comedies, and cheerful dramas, Hollywood began to change around 1940. That year Charlie Chaplin (1889–1977) released *The Great Dictator,* his satire on the rise of German dictator Adolf Hitler (1889–1945). In July 1941, *Sergeant York* opened. The story of a reluctant American war hero, *Sergeant York* was an obvious call for the United States to enter the war. It was later used by the military in a recruitment campaign. Isolationists, or people who wanted the United States to stay out of the war, attacked Hollywood's enthusiasm for entering the conflict. But congressional hearings into the matter did not help the isolationists. As Republican presidential hopeful Wendell Willkie (1892–1944) pointed out, 95 percent of Hollywood's output was nonpolitical. This other, nonpolitical Hollywood fare included Disney's classic animated film *Fantasia,* released in 1940. Movie studios continued to turn out lightweight comedies and romances even after America had entered the war.

In December 1941, just ten days after the bombing of Pearl Harbor, President Roosevelt (1882–1945) took steps to encourage Hollywood to make movies to help the war effort. The studios cooperated by producing pro-American movies such as *Casablanca* (1942). By the middle of 1942, around seventy war-related films had been made. Screenwriters gave existing scripts, and even partially finished movies, a wartime makeover. Gangsters became Nazi spies, while Tarzan took on German invaders. The Japanese were shown as cruel and vicious brutes.

The Office of War Information (OWI) was set up to coordinate the propaganda effort (propaganda is information used to persuade people of the government's position). Its head, Nelson Poynter (1903–1978), was concerned about the simplistic way Hollywood was dealing with the war. He wanted more positive films showing "good" Germans resisting the

Nazis. The OWI manual urged filmmakers to ask themselves: "Will this picture help win the war?" The OWI exerted pressure on Hollywood by refusing overseas distribution to movies that did not meet the manual's guidelines. Since Hollywood depended on overseas sales to make a profit, following the OWI manual made good business sense.

While Hollywood as a whole joined in the war effort with its pro-American movies, many individual filmmakers also did what they could to help. Director Frank Capra (1897–1991) enlisted in the army and went to work making documentaries. Capra's first film in a series, *Prelude to War,* won the Best Documentary Oscar in 1942. Other directors, such as John Ford (1895–1973), did similar work. But John Huston (1906–1987) fell afoul of the army's rules when he made *Let There Be Light* (1946), a film about shell-shocked veterans. Many actors also enlisted in the armed forces. James Stewart (1908–1997) and Douglas Fairbanks Jr. (1909–2000) joined up within weeks of Pearl Harbor. Frank Sinatra (1915–1998), who was declared unfit for military service because of a punctured eardrum, had to work hard to win back his movie fans after the war ended.

Besides joining in the war effort, filmmakers began to make a new kind of movie in the 1940s. A surprise hit of 1941 was *The Maltese Falcon,* an adaptation of a novel by Dashiell Hammett (1894–1961). Within a few years, these dark, cynical detective movies had a name: *film noir.* Noir films are shadowy, dark, and bleak, both in visual look and subject matter. America after the war seemed to be a prosperous, optimistic place. Yet *film noir* reflected a worry that things were not as good as they seemed. The cold war (an ideological war between the United States and the former Soviet Union) began just after World War II ended, bringing with it fears of nuclear war. Americans were afraid of a Communist takeover. But they also worried that their own government could not be trusted. Movies such as *The Big Sleep* (1946), *The Killers* (1946), and *Out of the Past* (1947) describe these fears.

Hollywood in the 1940s had good cause to feel threatened. Despite the popularity of film noir, attendance at movie theaters was falling steadily. To make matters worse for the major studios, the U.S. Justice Department ended the studios' total control of film distribution. Then, in May 1947, the House Un-American Activities Committee (HUAC) accused Hollywood of harboring subversives. Many people were ordered to appear at congressional hearings to make statements about their political views. Dalton Trumbo (1905–1976) and John Howard Lawson (1894–1977) were among ten writers and directors, referred to as the Hollywood Ten, who refused to cooperate with the "witch hunt." They, and many others, were blacklisted, which meant they were not allowed to work in the movie

When *The Maltese Falcon* appeared in 1941, it was the third time Dashiell Hammett's novel had been turned into a movie. The previous two attempts were disastrous failures. At first, this try did not look much like a hit either. It was made by first-time director John Huston (1906–1987) with a low-budget cast. Humphrey Bogart (1899–1957), soon to become a major star, was then just another gangster movie regular. Sidney Greenstreet (1879–1954) was over sixty years old and acting in his first movie. Mary Astor (1906–1987) was trying to rebuild a career that had been ruined by scandal in the 1930s. Peter Lorre (1904–1964) had worked for years in minor character parts. But this Warner Brothers "B"-movie (a name given to low-budget movies) was to become one of the all-time great films. Often referred to as the first real *film noir, The Maltese Falcon* is also one of the finest movies of that genre. Besides making stars of Bogart, Greenstreet, Astor, and Lorre, it helped change the face of American filmmaking in the 1940s.

industry. Hollywood's image was damaged by the controversy, but many of the so-called Hollywood Ten eventually did work there again. Blacklisted writers, including Trumbo, submitted screenplays under different names, and studio bosses turned a blind eye.

❖ MUSIC TAKES IN SWING AND SILENCE

The 1940s were dynamic years for American music. Electric instruments revolutionized the blues, bebop shook up jazz, and even classical music experimented with new sounds. Musicians challenged existing styles or fused them to make new music. The arrival of European composers, who were fleeing the Nazis in Germany, had a huge influence on classical music and on movie soundtracks. Improved recording techniques and new, affordable technology meant that music was beginning to accompany everyday life.

Swing was the soundtrack for World War II. Developed in the 1930s, by 1940 swing was everywhere, from 78-rpm (revolutions per minute) records played in homes, to dance halls, the movies, and on the radio.

*Jazz musicians like
Charlie Parker produced a
new style of jazz, called
bebop, during the 1940s.
Parker was one of the
most influential and
popular of the 1940s jazz
artists.* **Reproduced by
permission of the
Corbis Corporation.**

Some big bands were led by solo musicians such as trumpeter Louis Armstrong (1901–1971) and clarinetist Benny Goodman (1909–1986). Other bands toured the country fronted by singers such as Billie Holiday (1915–1959) and Frank Sinatra (1915–1998). In the second half of the decade, swing declined in popularity. Perry Como (1912–2001), Vaughn Monroe (1911–1973), and others fronted a toned-down swing sound, heavy with stringed instruments.

But even as swing was losing its appeal, some musicians began turning it into a more serious kind of music. Duke Ellington (1899–1974) was probably the most influential. Ellington became a respected composer, but others, such as Gil Evans (1912–1988) and Count Basie (1904–1984), also explored new sounds and instruments. Classical composers, meanwhile, turned to jazz. Igor Stravinsky (1882–1971) wrote the *Ebony Concerto* for the Woody Herman big band. American composer Aaron Copland (1900–1990) wrote music for clarinet player and band leader Benny Goodman (1909–1986).

In the nightclubs, a stripped-down, high-speed kind of jazz called bebop was emerging. Small combos of four or five players beat out undanceable rhythms and meandering riffs. Lester Young (1909–1959)

Dancing Down Broadway

Jazz dance and tap dancing were an important part of Broadway musicals and musical films. In the 1940s, around eleven million people each year attended Broadway shows such as *Oklahoma!* (1943), *Anchors Aweigh* (1945), and *Annie Get Your Gun* (1946). Choreographers such as Helen Tamiris (1905–1966) worked with composer Richard Rodgers (1902–1979), while Jerome Robbins (1918–1998) choreographed *On the Town* (1944), the influential musical by Leonard Bernstein (1918–1990). In the movies, dancers Fred Astaire (1899–1987) and Gene Kelly (1912–1996) became stars. Some of the most spectacular dance routines of the century were captured in such movies as *Holiday Inn* (1942) and the film version of *On the Town* (1949).

and Theodore "Fats" Navarro (1923–1950) were leading bebop players. But the top performer in the new style was Charlie Parker (1920–1955), sometimes known as "Bird." Parker's wild saxophone improvisations turned tunes such as "Scrapple from the Apple" and "Ornithology" into jazz masterpieces. In 1947, Parker's quintet featured an outstanding young trumpeter named Miles Davis (1926–1991) who went on to create "Cool Jazz," the defining jazz sound of the 1950s.

Like jazz, the blues was a musical style undergoing changes in the 1940s. Black blues musicians moved north to cities such as Chicago, Illinois. There they turned the reflective, acoustic blues of the rural South into a punchy, loud, electrified urban sound. Blues performers such as Muddy Waters (1915–1983) and Sam "Lightnin'" Hopkins (1912–1982) would directly influence rock and roll during the 1950s. The use of electric tape recording meant that all kinds of music could be heard in all sorts of places. Blues merged with jazz, jazz merged with country and western. From this eclectic mix came new musical styles such as rhythm and blues, boogie-woogie, and honky-tonk.

The experience of rural folk living in the city was a feature of country music in the 1940s. Country-swing bands, such as Bob Wills and the Texas Playboys, were popular in urban centers throughout the country, including Chicago; Los Angeles, California; and Mobile, Alabama. Gradually the lines between country, folk, and pop music dissolved. Pop singer

American Television Entertains

In the 1940s, it cost around ten times more to produce a program for television than for radio. But wartime limits on new broadcasting stations gave manufacturers the chance to improve television technology. As more and more Americans bought television sets, it became clear that TV would be a lucrative future market. In 1941, there were only around fifteen thousand television receivers in the United States. By 1950, there were eleven million. Radio networks transferred many of their popular programs to TV. Comedies such as *Our Miss Brooks* and *Amos and Andy* were early examples. Sports television broadcasts were popular, as were children's shows such as *Superman*. But the most popular television show of the 1940s was the *Texaco Star Theater,* a variety show starring Milton Berle (1908–2001). In 1948, 94.7 percent of television viewers tuned in to watch "Uncle Miltie."

Bing Crosby (1904–1977) recorded "Sioux City Sue," a popular country song. Bluegrass brought to country music an edge similar to the effect bebop had on jazz, while country and folk music each became more cynical, melancholy, and regretful. Gospel was a popular alternative to country and a big moneymaker for record companies in the 1940s. Gospel stars such as Mahalia Jackson (1911–1972) sold millions of records.

As in jazz, blues, and country, American classical composers began to experiment with new sounds in the 1940s. In the first three decades of the century, European composers had created music that was difficult and unsettling. Then in the late 1930s and early 1940s, many of these Europeans moved to the United States. Composers such as Arnold Schoenberg (1874–1951), Kurt Weill (1900–1950), and Igor Stravinsky (1882–1971) all had a profound influence on American music. American composer John Cage (1912–1992) was a pupil of Schoenberg. He was interested in the music of percussion, ordinary sounds, and silence. His experiments in the 1940s led directly to his most famous piece, "4'33" (four minutes and thirty-three seconds of silence), released in 1952.

❖ AMERICAN THEATER DOWNSIZES

Broadway theater audiences increased in the 1940s. But overall, play-going audiences turned away from drama during the decade. The political campaigning dramas of the 1930s seemed irrelevant in the face of world war. After 1945, plays were made on a smaller scale. They focused on family life and on individuals struggling with inner conflict. Personal life, rather than political struggle, was the subject of most 1940s drama.

Noted playwright Tennessee Williams (1914–1983) wrote two of the most important plays of the decade. *The Glass Menagerie* (1945) was his first. Characters in this play have romantic hopes and dreams for the future, but their reality is brutal and bleak. In many ways, the mood of Williams's plays matched the *film noir* trend in the movies. *A Streetcar Named Desire* (1947), considered his masterpiece, depicts the interaction between characters who are all intense, frustrated, and bitter about their lives. Williams's plays are always full of illusion and disappointment.

Arthur Miller (1915–) also produced two classics of American literature in the 1940s. Miller took Williams's view of personal failure and disillusionment a step further. He attacked capitalism (the economic system of the United States), suggesting that American life can end only in personal loss and failure. Both *All My Sons* (1947) and the Pulitzer Prize-winning *Death of a Salesman* (1949) show the American Dream to be an illusion. Because of these plays, Miller was branded an anti-American. He was one of the most prominent figures to be questioned by the House Un-American Activities Committee during the 1950s.

Television became extremely popular in the 1940s due to improvements in technology and increased programming. *Reproduced by permission of AP/Wide World Photos.*

Besides these two rising stars, established playwrights such as Lillian Hellman (1906–1984) and Eugene O'Neill (1888–1953) continued to produce important work. O'Neill's *The Iceman Cometh* (1946), in particular, was highly acclaimed. But on the whole, drama on and around Broadway was bland and unexciting in the 1940s. Off Broadway, however, the story was different. In small theaters, high school halls, and other small spaces, drama workshops thrived. For example, future movie star Marlon Brando (1924–) began his career with Erwin Piscator's Drama Workshop. Although big productions had lost their edge, small-scale drama continued to keep its audiences interested.

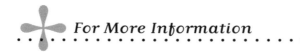 *For More Information*

BOOKS

Awmiller, Craig. *This House on Fire: The Story of the Blues*. New York: Franklin Watts, 1996.

Bailey, Donna. *Dancing*. Austin, TX: Raintree Steck-Vaughn Library, 1991.

Balliett, Whitney. *American Musicians: Fifty Portraits in Jazz*. New York: Oxford University Press, 1986.

Barnes, Rachel. *Abstract Expressionists*. Chicago, IL: Heinemann Library, 2002.

Benton, Mike. *The Comic Book in America: An Illustrated History*. Dallas, TX: Taylor, 1989.

Bredeson, Carmen. *American Writers of the 20th Century*. Springfield, NJ: Enslow Publishers, 1996.

Chronicle of the Twentieth Century. Mount Cisco, NY: Chronicle Books, 1994.

Decade of Triumph: The 40s. Alexandria, VA: Time-Life Books, 1999.

Dunning, John. *Tune in Yesterday: The Ultimate Encyclopedia of Old-Time Radio 1925–1976*. Englewood Cliffs, NJ: Prentice-Hall, 1976.

Faber, Doris, and Harold Faber. *American Literature*. New York: Atheneum Books for Young Readers, 1995.

Fariello, Griffin. *Red Scare: Memories of the American Inquisition, An Oral History*. New York: Norton, 1995.

Feinstein, Stephen. *The 1940s from World War II to Jackie Robinson*. Berkeley Heights, NJ: Enslow Publishers, 2000.

Freedman, Russell. *Martha Graham: A Dancer's Life*. New York: Clarion Books, 1998.

Goulart, Ron. *Comic Book Culture: An Illustrated History*. Portland, OR: Collector's Press, 2000.

Hart, James David, and Philip Leininger, eds. *The Oxford Companion to American Literature*. New York: Oxford University Press, 1995.

Hatch, Shari Dorantes, and Michael R. Strickland, eds. *African-American Writers: A Dictionary.* Santa Barbara, CA: ABC-CLIO, 2000.

Hills, Ken. *1940s.* Austin, TX: Raintree Steck-Vaughn, 1992.

Jacobs, Jay. *The Color Encyclopedia of World Art.* New York: Crown Publishers, 1975

Janson, H. W. *History of Art.* New York: Abrams, 1995.

Jones, Hettie. *Big Star Fallin' Mama: Five Women in Black Music.* New York: Viking, 1995.

Jordan, Matt Dukes. *Swankyville: A Guide to All That Swings.* Los Angeles: General Pub. Group, 1999

Karl, Frederick R. *American Fictions, 1940–1980.* New York: Harper and Row, 1983.

Manchel, Frank. *Women on the Hollywood Screen.* New York: Franklin Watts, 1977.

Margolick, David. *Strange Fruit: Billie Holiday, Cafe Society, and an Early Cry for Civil Rights.* Philadelphia: Running Press, 2000.

McGilligan, Pat, ed. *Backstory 2: Interviews with Screenwriters of the 1940s and 1950s.* Berkeley, CA: University of California Press, 1991.

Oermann, Robert K. *A Century of Country: An Illustrated History of Country Music.* New York: TV Books, 1999.

Pease, Esther E. *Modern Dance.* Dubuque, IA: W.C. Brown Co., 1976.

Porter, James A. *Modern Negro Art.* New York: Dryden Press, 1943.

Schatz, Thomas. *Boom and Bust: American Cinema in the 1940s.* Berkeley, CA: University of California Press, 1999.

Silver, Alain, and Elizabeth Ward. *Film Noir: An Encyclopedic Reference to the American Style.* Woodstock, NY: Overlook Press, 1992.

Simon, Charman. *Hollywood at War: The Motion Picture Industry and World War II.* New York: Franklin Watts, 1995.

Smith, Dian G. *Great American Film Directors: From the Flickers Through Hollywood's Golden Age.* New York: J. Messner, 1987.

Spiegelman, Art, and Chip Kidd. *Jack Cole and Plastic Man: Forms Stretched to Their Limits.* Mount Cisco, NY: Chronicle Books, 2001.

Spring, Justin. *The Essential Jackson Pollock.* New York: Wonderland Press, Harry N. Abrams, 1998.

Strubel, John Warthen. *The History of American Classical Music.* New York: Facts on File, 1995.

Terrace, Vincent. *The Complete Encyclopedia of Television Programs 1947–1979.* New York: Barnes, 1980.

Tucker, Sherrie. *Swing Shift: "All-Girl" Bands of the 1940s.* Durham: Duke University Press, 2000.

Turner, Jane, ed. *The Dictionary of Art.* New York: Grove, 1996.

Wilds, Mary. *Raggin' the Blues: Legendary Country, Blues, and Ragtime Musicians.* Greensboro, NC: Avisson Press, 2001.

Wood, Tim, and R. J. Unstead. *The 1940s.* New York: Franklin Watts, 1990.

WEB SITES

American Cultural History: 1940–1949. [Online] http://www.nhmccd.edu/contracts/lrc/kc/decade40.html#film (accessed March 2002).

Film Noir. [Online] http://www.filmsite.org/filmnoir.html (accessed March 2002).

The Timley Comics Story. [Online] http://www.geocities.com/Athens/Olympus/7160/Timely1.htm (accessed March 2002).

chapter two *Business and the Economy*

1940: **January 9** In Chicago, a federal circuit court rules that Inland Steel Corporation does not have to recognize the Steel Workers' Organizing Committee as the sole agent for bargaining with workers.

1940: **October 24** The forty-hour workweek begins, two years after it was passed as part of the Fair Labor Standards Act of 1938.

1941: **January 3** The federal government orders the construction of two hundred merchant ships in preparation for the possibility of entering World War II.

1941: **January 7** The Office of Production Management is set up to supervise defense production. William S. Knudsen is put in charge.

1941: **April 11** For the first time, the Ford Motor Company signs a deal with unions to end a strike involving 85,000 workers.

1941: **May 16** U.S. Defense Savings Bonds go on sale to raise money for defense efforts.

1941: **December 7** The Japanese sneak attack on Pearl Harbor, Hawaii, leads President Roosevelt to declare war.

1941: **December 27** The Office of Price Administration and Civilian Supply (OPA), established in April, introduces rubber rationing. Civilian rubber consumption drops by 80 percent.

1942: **January 16** The Office of Production Management (OPM) is replaced by the War Production Board. It is a sign that the nation is now on a war footing.

1942: **January 30** President Roosevelt signs the Price Control Bill. This bill sets prices for all products except farm goods.

1942: **May 5** Sugar rationing is introduced.

1942: **May 15** Gasoline is rationed in seventeen eastern states. Each driver is allowed only three gallons per week for nonessential journeys.

1943: **March 29** Meat, fat, and cheese join coffee, sugar, and canned goods on the list of products subject to government rationing.

1943: **May 1** The federal government takes over the nation's mines to end a strike by 530,000 miners. In December, the government will also take over the railroads for similar reasons.

1943: **June 20** When African Americans are brought into war industries, race riots break out in Detroit. In two days, thirty-five people are killed and five hundred are wounded, most of them black.

1944: **January 19** The railways are returned to their owners by the federal government.

1944: **May 3** The OPA ends meat rationing except for steak and other choice cuts.

1944: **July** At the Bretton Woods Conference, held in New Hampshire, international diplomats set up the World Bank, International Monetary Fund

(IMF), and the General Agreement on Tariffs and Trade (GATT).

1944: **August 14** Manufacturers are allowed to begin making consumer goods again.

1945: **May 7** Germany officially surrenders to the Allies.

1945: **August 15** Rationing of oil and gasoline ends.

1945: **August 18** President Harry S Truman orders the return of free markets and the end of war production.

1946: In a record year for labor disputes, strikes disrupt many industries, including steel, automobiles, mining, railroads, and shipping. In Philadelphia in August, strikes shut off the supply of bread.

1946: **October 19** Loans to foreign countries under the Lend-Lease scheme reach $51 billion.

1946: **November 29** After calling 400,000 miners out on strike against government orders, John L. Lewis, leader of the United Mine Workers Union, is indicted for contempt of court.

1947: **January 7** After a distinguished wartime career as an army general, George C. Marshall is named U.S. Secretary of State.

1947: **April 7** In the first nationwide telephone strike, 300,000 communication workers walk off their jobs.

1947: **May 9** The World Bank loans France $250 million to help reconstruct its industries and cities.

1947: **May 13** The Taft-Hartley Act puts limits on labor union powers.

1947: **June 11** Sugar rationing ends.

1947: **November 8** Under the Marshall Plan, the U.S. government proposes to give European countries $17 billion to help reconstruct their economies.

1948: **February 10** The Congress of Industrial Organizations (CIO) ejects all members opposed to the Marshall Plan.

1948: **June 21** The U.S. Supreme Court rules that unions may not be prevented from publishing political opinions.

1948: **August 16** Americans are buying mass amounts of consumer goods on credit. In order to slow down the economy and control inflation, the Federal Reserve increases interest rates.

1948: **November 15** The first American-built electric locomotive is tested by General Electric and the American Locomotive Company.

1949: **January 14** An antitrust lawsuit is filed by the U.S. Department of Justice against the American Telephone and Telegraph Company (AT&T). The suit argues that AT&T's telephone network should be separate from its manufacturing subsidiary, Western Electric.

1949: **February 25** For the first time since the war, General Motors cuts the price of automobiles.

Overview

At the end of the 1930s, the American economy was still struggling with unemployment, militant labor unions, and a lack of demand for goods. But as Europe collapsed into conflict in 1939, the United States began to escape the effects of the Great Depression (1930–39). American businesses sold goods such as steel to European countries. When the allied nations (led by France and Great Britain) ran short of money, the Roosevelt administration funded their purchases of weapons, ships, and aircraft. In 1940, the U.S. government policy was one of helping the allied cause but avoiding direct involvement in the war. By supplying arms to the democratic countries, the United States hoped to become the "arsenal of democracy."

During the 1930s, Congress had heard evidence that big business had pushed the United States into World War I (1914–18) because bankers and arms manufacturers had wanted to protect their investments in Europe. By 1940, American involvement in another European war was unthinkable for most politicians. For many businesses, however, the European war was damaging their markets. They wanted to intervene. When the Japanese bombed the American fleet at Pearl Harbor on December 7, 1941, the policy of isolation disappeared overnight. Within weeks, American businesses had begun full-scale wartime production.

For almost a decade, the Roosevelt administration had been wary of big business. But after the attack on Pearl Harbor, business leaders volunteered to work for the government. These "dollar a year" men kept their company salaries, but were paid a dollar a year as government consultants. By doing this, they managed to prevent the federal government from taking control of major industries. The federal government made deals with business to meet war needs. Agencies were set up to help control the kinds of goods being produced and to keep prices at reasonable levels. For example, munitions were ordered on a "cost plus" basis. This meant that manufacturers received their production costs plus a small profit agreed upon by all. The emphasis was on speed of production, not on efficiency. President Franklin D. Roosevelt said that he was changing his name from "Dr. New Deal" to "Dr. Win-the-War."

Wartime production levels finally put an end to the Great Depression. By 1946, unemployment was low, wages were at record levels, and the economy was booming. Labor shortages caused by the war meant that many women and teenagers had entered the labor market. Returning soldiers threatened to push unemployment back up after the war, but President Harry S Truman, Roosevelt's successor, used the GI Bill to put them through college instead. This eased the pressure on the economy and produced a better-educated workforce. Price controls imposed by the Office of Price Administration (OPA) ended on July 1, 1946. Almost immediately, prices jumped up, but this time American industry was ready to respond. Increased production of consumer goods pushed prices back down. In the postwar years, Americans bought huge numbers of cars, refrigerators, televisions, and other household appliances. The consumer age had begun.

Not everything about the postwar world was good for business, however. After the war, politicians and bankers tried to stop the world from being divided into economic areas closed to American trade. Several international agreements and organizations—The Marshall Plan, the World Bank, the International Monetary Fund (IMF), and the General Agreement on Tariffs and Trade (GATT)—were put in place to keep world markets open and to help the global economy recover. Unfortunately, the former Soviet Union refused to help with any rebuilding that had strings attached. It absorbed several countries of Eastern Europe to form a closed economic area isolated behind the so-called Iron Curtain. The scene was set for the cold war, a forty-year nonmilitary standoff between western nations and the Soviet Union.

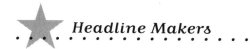

Elizabeth Arden (1884–1966) As one of the first women to reach a high level in American business, Elizabeth Arden realized early in her career that in order to succeed she would have to open her own cosmetics salon. By the 1930s, she had a chain of salons with locations throughout North and South America and Europe. She encouraged women employees to aim for promotion within the business. During the 1940s, sales of Elizabeth Arden products topped $60 million annually. When she died, Arden bequeathed $4 million to be divided equally among her employees. *Photo reproduced by permission of AP/Wide World Photos.*

William Edward Boeing (1881–1956) In 1915, William Edward Boeing created the Boeing Airplane Company, copying designs from planes used in Europe during World War I (1914–18). In the 1940s, his Seattle-area factories produced some of the most influential aircraft used in World War II (1939–45), including the B-29 Superfortress, used to drop the first atomic bomb on Japan. Boeing influenced the aviation industry as an innovator and enthusiast as well as a chief executive. His company went on to become one of the most powerful players in aviation worldwide. *Photo reproduced by permission of AP/Wide World Photos.*

Sidney Hillman (1887–1946) Sidney Hillman emigrated from Russia to the United States in 1907. He became president of the Amalgamated Clothing Workers of America in 1914, and by 1940 he was a close ally of the Roosevelt administration. His influence on labor policy during the 1930s and 1940s was considerable, but his position in government lost him the trust of labor unions. Hillman was passed over as a possible head of the War Manpower Commission when it was created in 1942. He suffered a heart attack not long afterward. He remained an influential Democratic Party insider until his death. *Photo reproduced by permission of the Corbis Corporation.*

Henry Kaiser (1882–1967) As an eighth-grade dropout in 1914, Henry Kaiser set up a company to build roads in the northwestern United States. His company was part of a consortium that built the Hoover Dam. During World War II, Kaiser's construction companies built almost everything from roads to shelters, but mostly they built ships. Kaiser's firms specialized in mass-produced "Liberty Ships," the basic wartime cargo carriers. The manufacturing emphasis was on speed, not quality. His shipyard in Vancouver, Washington built a ten-thousand-ton ship in just four-and-one-half days. By 1943, the company had received over $3 billion in government contracts. *Photo courtesy of the Library of Congress.*

John L. Lewis (1880–1969) John L. Lewis was responsible for bringing trade union membership to many workers who previously had been ignored by labor leaders. Unusually, Lewis had been a Republican since the 1920s. Most other labor leaders supported the Democrats, but in the 1940s the Republican Lewis became a powerful critic of the Democratic Roosevelt administration. After a series of damaging strikes, Lewis and his United Mine Workers (UMW) were heavily fined for breaking their non-strike promises. He retired as head of the UMW in 1960. *Photo courtesy of the U.S. Information Agency.*

Philip K. Wrigley (1894–1977) Philip K. Wrigley first worked in his father's soap factory, where he was a great success as a salesman. In the years leading up to the war, the company moved into chewing gum, pointing out how "healthful" its Doublemint gum was. During the war, with sugar rationed, Wrigley faced a supply problem. But he managed to persuade the military to include a stick of his gum in every soldier's ration pack, and the problem was solved. At home, he marketed his gum by saying that thirst and nicotine were agents of Hitler. By chewing gum to alleviate thirst and as an alternative to smoking, Americans were helping to fight fascism. *Photo reproduced by permission of the Corbis Corporation.*

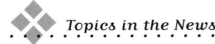

Topics in the News •

❖ WAR ENDS THE GREAT DEPRESSION

In 1939, the American economy was struggling. Unemployment was high, while prices and wages were low. By 1940, with Europe at war, everything had changed. European countries were desperate for goods to use in the war effort. They spent millions of dollars on American steel, ammunition, weapons, and food. Yet private businesses were slow to react to the demands of war. Many manufacturers continued to make consumer goods when military hardware was most needed. Shortages of raw materials also held up the recovery. Rather than issuing government orders or taking control of industries, the Roosevelt administration chose to guide private industry into producing what was required. It struck deals with private businesses to boost wartime production. This mixture of private money and federal incentives became the model for the American economy for the next thirty years.

In the 1930s, President Franklin D. Roosevelt (1882–1945) set up so many new government agencies, each known by a set of initials, that they collectively were known as "alphabet soup." Some of these agencies were converted to war work in the 1940s. But several new agencies were set up specifically to deal with the war. Headed by William S. Knudsen (1879–1948), the Office of Production Management (OPM) set production targets for raw materials such as steel. In 1941, the Supply Priorities and Allocations Board (SPAB) took on some of the OPM's duties. The National Defense Mediation Board (NDMB) tried to make sure essential industries were not disrupted by strikes. Early in 1942, the War Production Board (WPB) and the National War Labor Board (NWLB) became the two main agencies monitoring the supply of goods and raw materials. Donald Nelson (1888–1959), a former Sears Roebuck executive, was appointed head of the WPB, becoming the most powerful man in the economy.

Yet despite all these efforts to keep supplies steady, the war did create shortages. In order to make sure essential supplies were shared fairly, many items, including meat, sugar, butter, and canned goods, were rationed. Every U.S. citizen was given a book of stamps. These stamps had to be handed over by the customer when he or she bought rationed goods. Many suppliers made extra money by illegally selling rationed goods to customers who did not have enough stamps, charging them extra. Gasoline was also rationed, but in a different way. Every vehicle was rated A to E, and carried a sticker in the window with a letter on it. Those rated "A" were private automobiles, and were entitled to very little gas. Emergency

Despite the rationing system, supplies of certain consumer goods ran out during the war. Production of nylon stockings all but stopped when factories converted their operations to produce parachutes and medical supplies. Women took to drawing a line up the backs of their legs so that people would think they were wearing seamed stockings. Eyeglasses, usually imported from Germany, became very scarce. The federal government ran "scrap drives" to help save on raw materials. Children collected bacon fat (used in making ammunition), old newspapers (for recycling), old tin cans, tin foil, and other scrap metal. Scrap drives brought the nation together in the fight against fascism. But they had very limited effect on the shortages of consumer goods.

vehicles were rated "E," and could take as much as they needed. Others fell in between. Before long, there was a thriving black, or illegal, market in gasoline and other rationed goods.

Although there were still shortages at home, by 1943 the American economy was more productive than it had ever been. Between 1940 and 1945, American industry produced eighty-six thousand tanks, thirty thousand aircraft, and sixty-five hundred ships. U.S. Steel made twenty-one million helmets for the army. Quality improved as well. Aircraft could fly farther and faster than ever. The General-Purpose vehicle, known in soldier slang as the GP, or Jeep, grew tougher. Advances made during wartime helped American industry reach its dominant postwar position. By 1946, corporate America was desperate to separate Americans from the $140 billion they had saved in times of shortage and rationing. Keeping that spending under control was one of the biggest challenges faced by President Harry S Truman in the late 1940s.

❖ GOVERNMENT FINDS NEW WAYS TO FINANCE THE WAR

The American economy surged ahead in the early 1940s. This dramatic recovery resulted from massive federal spending on defense. The cost of U.S. involvement in the war, between 1941 and 1945, came in at a staggering $360 billion. Less than half of that was paid for by taxation. Instead, the federal government borrowed money to cover its wartime expense. In

Buying war bonds was
considered a patriotic act
on the part of American
citizens. The money from
the sales of the bonds
went to the government
to help with war costs.
*Courtesy of the National
Archives and Records
Administration.*

BUY WAR BONDS

1940, government debt stood at $43 billion. By 1945, the U.S. government owed $260 billion.

Taxation was the most reliable way of raising money. But increasing income taxes was politically risky. The Roosevelt administration had to be careful not to take too much money from ordinary Americans. This policy made sense not only because it kept voters supporting the Democratic president. The federal government also might have damaged the economy by reducing the amount of money American consumers had to spend if it had raised taxes too much. Instead, the administration opted for a "progressive" taxation system, in which people with higher incomes paid a progressively larger tax as a percentage of their income. Wartime tax policies were so successful that they continued until 1964.

The 1942 Revenue Act imposed the highest income taxation rates in American history. The highest earners paid a 91-percent tax on some of their income. Companies paid up to 40 percent of their gross profits in corporation taxes. Most significantly, however, more Americans were paying taxes than ever before. The number of taxpayers rose from 39 million in 1939 to 42.6 million in 1945. A new system for collecting taxes was put in place. Though it was meant as a temporary wartime arrangement, payroll deduction became routine after the war.

But even increased taxation still did not provide enough money to pay for the war. Sixty percent of the war's cost was met by borrowing. The main form of government borrowing was a system of war bonds. Americans could buy these bonds from the U.S. government in denominations from $25 up to $10,000. Bond holders could sell the investments back to the government at a later date. In total, $135 billion was raised by the sale of government war bonds. Most of the bonds were sold to banks and insurance companies looking for secure investments at a time of great uncertainty. But for ordinary Americans, buying war bonds became a patriotic act. Private citizens lent $36 billion to the nation through the war-bond system. Bond drives, some featuring publicity stunts, encouraged people to buy bonds. The horseshoes of Kentucky Derby winner Man o'War were auctioned off at a war-bond drive, while movie actress Hedy Lamarr (1913–2000) gave out kisses in exchange for buying bonds.

It was not just the war effort that benefited from this combination of progressive taxation and investment in bonds. The difference between rich and poor in America began to level out. In 1939, the top five percent of earners had 25 percent of the nation's disposable income. In 1945, they had only 17 percent. For the first time in American history, the rich had stopped getting richer. When the war ended, people cashed in their bonds and began spending the money on consumer goods. High wages, and America's domination of world trade, insured the emergence of a new American middle class after World War II.

The performance of the economy after the war soon helped reduce the federal deficit. In 1945, the federal government spent $53 billion more than it received in taxation. By 1950, federal spending outstripped income by only $3 billion. Government debt, however, did not go away. The amount

The Spruce Goose

Aviation enthusiast and movie tycoon Howard Hughes (1905–1976) made a fortune during World War II. His company built planes for the military. One of the planes that Hughes's company built was a huge aircraft which was half boat and half plane. The so-called "Spruce Goose," which was built mostly of birch, was so large that observers joked that a small plane could take off from its horizontal tail fins. The vertical tail fin towered 113 feet above the ground, equal to the length of a B-17 Flying Fortress bomber. The plane's 320-foot wingspan was the largest in aviation history. Hughes made a vow that either the Spruce Goose would fly or he would leave the country. On November 2, 1947, the eight three-thousand horse-power engines were fired up and, by some miracle, the Spruce Goose took to the air. It managed to fly one mile and landed in Long Beach harbor, never to fly again. Hughes did not have to leave the country. Although the whole affair was a great embarrassment for the government, the project proved the confidence and energy of American industry.

owed by the federal government dipped from $260 billion in 1945 to $256 billion in 1950, but it continued to climb for most of the next fifty years.

❖ COLD WAR TENSIONS CREATE THE "MILITARY-INDUSTRIAL COMPLEX"

Ever since the Russian revolution in 1917, political tension had existed between the United States and the Soviet Union. The two nations had come together to fight the Nazis during World War II, but after 1945 the Soviet Union hoped to expand its borders. This expansion threatened to close off many of the markets where American companies did business. After the war, President Harry S Truman decided that the spread of the Soviet Union had to be stopped. His adviser was George F. Kennan (1904–), an official at the American embassy in Moscow. Kennan's advice led to a foreign policy that would stay in place for the next forty-five years. It was known as the policy of "containment." The U.S. government wanted to "contain" the spread of Soviet power and influence.

Truman's containment policy was matched by aggressive talk from Moscow. In the late 1940s, the United States and the Soviet Union each

One of the reasons to stop the expansion of the Soviet Union was the effect such a development might have on trade. As World War II came to an end, American diplomats and business leaders tried to make sure there would be free markets around the world. In 1944, with the end of the war in sight, the Bretton Woods Agreement was signed. It set up two institutions, the International Monetary Fund (IMF) and the World Bank (International Bank of Reconstruction and Development), and established the General Agreement on Tariffs and Trade (GATT), a multilateral agreement that set rules for trade between countries. Because America had come out of the war without suffering damage at home, representatives from the United States dominated the IMF and the World Bank. Free trade was encouraged through GATT, and measures were put in place to regulate currency markets. The IMF lent money to governments to help them rebuild after the war. It charged interest on its loans.

began spending billions of dollars on defense and entered what was known as the cold war. The nonmilitary standoff earned the nickname because neither country wanted nor could afford a "hot" war with one another. Still, the Soviet Union and its Communist ideology seemed so threatening to world governments that one of the first things Truman did as president was to give $400 million to help Greece and Turkey fight Communist rebels. The United States did not want those two nations to become part of the Soviet Union.

In 1948, the Truman administration submitted a budget of $39.6 billion to Congress for approval. Around $18 billion, almost half of the total government spending, was earmarked for the military. For the first time in history, the United States began to build a large standing army. Just as it had between 1939 and 1945, such massive spending boosted American industry. The difference was that this time there was no sense that the war would ever end. A whole new kind of industry emerged, with the sole purpose of providing armaments, equipment, and ammunition for the Pentagon. Because it linked together the military and industry, this new part of the economy was known as the "military-industrial complex." By the end of the 1940s, it was one of the most powerful sectors of the American economy. During the 1940s, it seemed important that the military had a good supply of hardware. Very few people recognized the risk that such a powerful industry might want to keep the cold war going for its own benefit.

❖ AMERICAN BUSINESS MOVES INTO FOREIGN MARKETS

One of the causes of the Great Depression was the loss of access to foreign markets by American companies. During World War II American businesses expanded rapidly. They supplied billions of dollars' worth of goods to war-ravaged countries such as France and Great Britain. By the time the war ended, American businesses had built up huge reserves of money. In the late 1940s they used this money to invest abroad.

In 1947, the United States invested a total of $26.7 billion abroad. Sixteen billion dollars of that capital came from private companies. The rest came from the federal government in the form of loans and investments

American businesses expanded by promoting their products to the armed forces and to other nations. Reproduced by permission of the Corbis Corporation.

The 1940s saw the United States recover from the economic problems of the 1930s. In particular, it began to export more goods than it imported. This had not happened for almost a decade. The table shows the value of exported and imported goods in the 1940s.

Year	Exports ($000)	Imports ($000)	+/- ($000)
1940	4,030	7,433	-3,403
1941	5,153	4,375	+778
1942	8,081	3,113	+4,968
1943	13,028	3,511	+9,517
1944	15,345	4,066	+11,279
1945	10,097	4,280	+5,816
1946	9,996	5,533	+4,464
1947	14,674	7,904	+6,770
1948	12,967	9,176	+3,791
1949	12,160	7,467	+4,693

Source: U.S. Bureau of the Census, *Statistical Abstract of the United States: 1996.*

through such agencies as the World Bank, the International Monetary Fund (IMF), and the Reconstruction Finance Corporation (RFC). Part of the reason for this overseas investment was to stop the spread of communism. But the main aim of American spending overseas was to prevent another economic disaster like the Great Depression.

American business expansion in the 1940s often happened through joint ventures by U.S. companies with the federal government and with foreign governments. Some business leaders managed to expand into overseas markets and to be patriotic at the same time. Robert W. Woodruff (1889–1985), president of Coca-Cola, faced a serious problem during the war. With the supply of sugar rationed, his product was under threat. Woodruff solved the problem by convincing the government that soldiers and industrial workers would be better off if they drank Coca-Cola. Before long, wherever American troops went, they took Coca-Cola with them. In this way, Coca-Cola was introduced to a worldwide market and has stayed there ever since.

The search for natural resources such as oil, coal, and metal ores also drove international expansion. By the end of the war, American continental reserves of high-grade iron ore were running out. Bethlehem Steel Corporation spent $37.5 million developing iron ore deposits in Latin America. In Brazil, the M. A. Hanna Company opened up an iron ore supply of around 160 million tons. The Anaconda Copper Mining Company invested $150 million in Chilean copper mines. Manufacturers also expanded onto foreign soil. Ford invested $3 million to begin building cars in Australia, as did General Motors.

But it was oil that offered the biggest opportunity for expansion overseas. Every American oil company looked abroad for new reserves and new business in the 1940s. U.S. Secretary of the Interior Harold Ickes (1874–1952) helped American companies gain access to Middle Eastern oil reserves. This was often achieved through joint agreements with foreign companies and governments. Standard Oil, the most aggressive of the oil companies, spent $100 million building refineries, pipelines, and even new towns in Venezuela and elsewhere. It spent another $140 million on refineries in England. In all cases, the oil companies worked closely with the federal government. During the 1940s there was unprecedented cooperation between government and business. Nowhere was this more important than in overseas expansion.

❖ AMERICAN AID HELPS REBUILD EUROPE

In the aftermath of World War II, the nations of Europe faced terrible hardships. Major cities such as Berlin, Dresden, and Cologne in Germany and Coventry, Hull, and Liverpool in Great Britain had been flattened by bombs. To make matters worse, factories, railroads, ports, and major industries were severely damaged. In June 1947, U.S. Secretary of State George Marshall (1880–1959) proposed a program of aid to help rebuild several European nations. The program became known as the Marshall Plan.

Marshall and his supporters in Washington, D.C., believed that World War II had two causes. First, they believed that the United States had been mistaken in trying to keep out of international affairs after World War I. The United States had refused to join the League of Nations (a body set up to promote dialogue among countries), and it also had withdrawn from European affairs in the 1930s. The second cause of World War II, according to Marshall's supporters, was the failure of the United States to deal with war debts after World War I. Heavy debts brought economic crisis to Germany in the 1920s and led to Adolf Hitler (1889–1945) and the Nazis taking power in 1933. The Marshall Plan aimed to prevent the same thing from happening again.

At first the Soviet Union, as well as other European nations, were keen to benefit from the Marshall Plan. But after the first meeting, the Soviets and their allies pulled out, claiming that the conditions attached to any aid would be unfair. Sixteen European nations stayed at the table. They eventually agreed to receive an aid package of $17 billion over four years. Five billion dollars would be paid in the first year. In return for providing aid, Marshall's supporters wanted to regulate the European economy just as the Roosevelt administration had regulated the American economy during the 1930s.

The federal government was eager to use the Marshall Plan to create a market free from trade barriers within Europe. There were several reasons this seemed important. Many European countries, including France and Italy, had developed powerful Communist parties, and many Americans worried that Soviet power would spread across Western Europe, just as fascism had done twenty years earlier. American businesses wanted Europe restored so that its citizens could buy more American goods. But whatever the motives, the Marshall Plan speeded the recovery of European nations and helped to avoid another economic crisis. It also laid the foundations for the European Common Market and the single currency called the Euro, which is now used in several western European countries.

❖ LABOR UNIONS EXERCISE POWER AND INFLUENCE

At no other time in American history have labor unions been as powerful as they were in the 1940s. During World War II, union membership grew rapidly. In 1941, 10.1 million workers belonged to labor unions. Four years later, 14.7 million men and women were union members. Labor unions had close ties with the Democratic Party and were supported in the president's cabinet by Secretary of Labor Frances Perkins (1882–1965). Their influence on federal government went far beyond their ability to organize strikes and protests.

Two large organizations dominated the labor movement: the American Federation of Labor (AFL) and the Congress of Industrial Organizations (CIO). Both unions agreed not to press for strikes while the war continued. But labor leaders soon became unhappy with the National War Labor Board (NWLB), the federal agency set up to control wages. They were also concerned that the NWLB and other wartime agencies were run by big business.

By 1942, trouble was brewing between big business and the labor unions. The cost of everyday household items was rising fast, and the unions demanded higher wages for their members. Eventually the NWLB agreed to a 15-percent pay increase. But by 1943, strikes were also on the increase. Over three million workers walked out on strike that year. The United Mine Workers' (UMW) leader John L. Lewis led four hundred thousand coal miners out on strike, breaking the no-strike deal. The strike was very unpopular with the general public, because coal was the main form of heating fuel. Lewis quickly became the most hated man in America.

Labor unions in general, and Lewis in particular, had enjoyed a close relationship with the Roosevelt administration. By 1943, everything had changed. There was talk of mines being seized by the federal government. Congress passed the War Labor Disputes Act, trying to make it illegal to encourage strikes in government-run plants. President Franklin D. Roosevelt stopped the bill, but ordered Secretary of the Interior Harold Ickes to take over the mines. Eventually a new way of calculating wages ended the dispute without breaking the NWLB rules regarding wage increases.

Labor unions were extremely powerful during the 1940s. Strikes, such as this Massachusetts dockworkers strike, helped union members gain better wages and working conditions. Reproduced by permission of the Corbis Corporation.

As worker shortages grew worse, Roosevelt looked for creative ways to solve the problem. In January 1944, he proposed making it possible for the federal government to order citizens to work anywhere it saw fit. The labor unions were angered by this plan. They saw it as a form of slave labor. And they had an unlikely friend in big business. Business leaders did not want to be told whom they should hire.

In 1946, not long after the end of the war, strikes broke out in the automobile, steel, communications, and electrical industries. This was a record year for walkouts in America, with 4.6 million workers setting down their tools. President Harry S Truman struggled with powerful unions that refused to accept wage settlements. In the end, the Truman administration took over mines and railroads. Still, the strikes went on, with Truman denouncing strikers as traitors. The UMW was heavily fined for violating a federal injunction. Yet, despite these conflicts, by the end of the decade growing prosperity had closed the rift between the Democratic administration and organized labor.

For More Information

BOOKS

Cayton, Andrew, Elizabeth I. Perry, and Allan M. Winkler. *America: Pathways to the Present: America in the Twentieth Century.* New York: Prentice Hall School Group, 1998.

Collier, Christopher. *Progressivism, the Great Depression, and the New Deal, 1901 to 1941.* New York: Benchmark Books/Marshall Cavendish, 2000.

Cook, Chris, and David Waller, eds. *The Longman Handbook of Modern American History, 1763–1996.* New York: Longman, 1998.

Decade of Triumph: The 40s. Alexandria, VA: Time-Life Books, 1999.

Donovan, Robert J. *The Second Victory: The Marshall Plan and the Postwar Revival of Europe.* New York: Madison Books, 1987.

Engerman, Stanley L., and Robert E. Gallman, eds. *The Cambridge Economic History of the United States: The Twentieth Century (Vol 3).* Cambridge, MA: Cambridge University Press, 2000.

Gordon, Lois, et al. *American Chronicle: Year by Year through the Twentieth Century.* New Haven, CT: Yale University Press, 1999.

Gould, William. *Boeing.* London: Cherrytree, 1995.

Gould, William. *Coca-Cola.* London: Cherrytree, 1995.

Isaacs, Sally Senzell. *America in the Time of Franklin Delano Roosevelt: The Story of Our Nation from Coast to Coast, from 1929 to 1948.* Des Plaines, IL: Heinemann Library, 2000.

Isaacs, Sally Senzell. *The Rise to World Power, 1929 to 1948.* Des Plaines, IL: Heine-mann Library, 1999.

Keylin, Arleen, and Jonathan Cohen, eds. *The Forties.* New York: Arno Press, 1980.

Larsen, Rebecca. *Franklin D. Roosevelt: Man of Destiny.* New York: Franklin Watts, 1991.

Lee, Bruce, ed. *Roosevelt and Marshall: The War They Fought, the Change They Wrought.* New York: HarperTrade, 1991.

Leonard, Thomas M. *Day by Day: The Forties.* New York: Facts on File, 1977.

May, George S., ed. *Encyclopedia of American Business History and Biography: Banking and Finance, 1913–1989.* New York: Facts on File, 1990.

May, Elaine Tyler. *Homeward Bound: American Families in the Cold War Era.* New York: Basic Books, 1988.

McCauley, Martin. *The Origins of the Cold War 1941–1949* (Seminar Studies in History). New York: Addison Wesley, 1996.

Schraff, Anne E. *The Great Depression and the New Deal: America's Economic Collapse and Recovery.* New York: Franklin Watts, 1990.

Schuman, Michael A. *Harry S Truman.* New York: Enslow, 1997.

Seely, Bruce, ed. *Encyclopedia of American Business History and Biography: Iron and Steel in the Twentieth Century.* New York: Facts on File, 1993.

Terkel, Studs. *The Good War: An Oral History of World War Two.* New York: Pantheon Books, 1984.

WEB SITES

Ad Access: Brief History of World War Two Advertising Campaigns. [Online] http://scriptorium.lib.duke.edu/adaccess/wwad-history.html (accessed March 2002).

America from the Great Depression to World War II: Photographs from the FSA-OWI, 1935–1945. [Online] http://memory.loc.gov/ammem/fsahtml/fahome. html (accessed March 2002).

FDR Library and Digital Archives: K12 Learning Center. [Online] http://www. fdrlibrary.marist.edu/teach.html (accessed March 2002).

George C. Marshall Foundation. [Online] http://www.marshallfoundation.org/ about_gcm/marshall_plan.htm (accessed March 2002).

National Records and Archives Administration: The Marshall Plan. [Online] http://www.nara.gov/exhall/featured-document/marshall/marshall.html (accessed March 2002).

Spruce Goose Exhibition. [Online] http://www.aero.com/museums/evergreen/ evergrn.htm (accessed March 2002).

Truman Presidential Museum and Library. [Online] http://www.trumanlibrary. org/index.html (accessed March 2002).

chapter three *Education*

1940: Ten million adults are listed as illiterate (unable to read or write) by the United States census.

1940: June The U.S. Supreme Court rules that any child who refuses to salute the American flag should be expelled from school.

1941: July 1 College students are no longer allowed to defer being drafted into the military.

1941: July At the University of Georgia, the pro-equality dean of education is fired by state governor Gene Talmadge. The firing leads to many faculty resignations, and the university loses its accreditation.

1941: December 16 In a scheme to help students graduate before reaching the military draft age of twenty-one, liberal arts colleges begin offering three-year degrees. These accelerated programs include classes taken during the summer.

1942: The U.S. Armed Forces Institute, based at the University of Wisconsin-Madison, begins offering correspondence courses.

1942: January The College Entrance Examination Board overhauls its testing methods. Instead of taking the traditional essay test, students begin taking tests measuring reading ability, problem-solving skills, and general knowledge.

1942: July It is estimated that there is a shortage of fifty thousand teachers in the United States.

1943: The U.S. Supreme Court reverses its decision to allow schools to expel students who refuse to salute the flag.

1943: April U.S. Education Commissioner John W. Studebaker promotes education for African Americans.

1943: November President Franklin D. Roosevelt proposes the Vocational Rehabilitation Act, later to become the GI Bill of Rights, the goal of which is to provide education for soldiers returning from military service.

1944: The American Armed Forces Institute offers 275 courses to war veterans.

1944: The Progressive Education Association changes its name to the American Education Fellowship.

1944: June 22 The Servicemen's Readjustment Act is signed into law by President Roosevelt.

1944: October 3–4 A conference on rural education is sponsored by the White House. It aims to find out whether the federal government could fund local education through state governments.

1945: June Virginia allocates $1.2 million to produce educational movies for public school students. The project is inspired by the success of the military in using films to educate soldiers.

1945: **September** The University of Maryland makes American history a compulsory part of its undergraduate curriculum.

1945: **November 1–16** The United Nations Educational, Scientific, and Cultural Organization (UNESCO) is founded.

1946: The U.S. Armed Forces Institute has enrolled eight hundred thousand veterans in correspondence courses. Fifty-three percent of students in residential college courses are war veterans.

1946: **July** The National Education Association announces that three hundred and fifty thousand teachers have left the profession since 1941.

1946: **July 30** President Harry S Truman signs a bill allowing the United States to participate in UNESCO.

1946: **August** Public Law 584, known as the Fulbright Act, is passed by Congress. The act provides assistance for students and academics to travel around the world to study in order to encourage cultural understanding.

1947: The cold war puts an end to many of UNESCOs educational programs in developing countries.

1947: **February 2** In Buffalo, New York, 2,400 teachers go on strike for higher pay. Governor Thomas E. Dewey will later make strikes by teachers illegal.

1947: **September** Seventy-five thousand students go without schooling nationwide because there are not enough teachers.

1947: **October** Separate education for blacks and whites is condemned by the President's Committee on Civil Rights.

1948: New Jersey desegregates its public schools. From now on, black and white students in New Jersey will study together.

1948: **March** In Minneapolis, Minnesota, there is a twenty-seven-day teachers' strike for higher wages.

1948: **March 8** In *McCollum* v. *Board of Education,* the U.S. Supreme Court outlaws religious education or activity in public schools.

1948: **April 1** Although the Senate passes a bill providing $300 million in federal education funding for the states, it is defeated in the U.S. House of Representatives.

1949: The New York state university system opens its first campus. It will eventually include thirty small institutions.

1949: The House Un-American Activities Commission (HUAC) requires that lists of books used in courses be submitted for inspection. The Commission is looking for Communist Party propaganda.

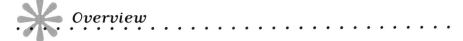

Overview

American education was transformed in the 1940s. At all levels it became better organized, better funded, and more standardized across the country. Universities were modernized. In subjects such as literature, history, and the arts, the college curriculum was made more professional and was more carefully thought out. The sciences took a higher profile than before. These changes in higher education soon filtered down to the public schools.

The main reason for these changes was World War II (1939–45). The war exposed many problems within American education. In total, the army rejected five million recruits, some because of poor health, but many because they could not read and write. The process of drafting army recruits showed that a person's ability to read, write, and do math depended on where in the country he or she grew up. College graduates also turned out to be of variable quality, and there were shortages of foreign-language and science specialists. Educators realized that something had to be done.

The war threw education into full-scale crisis. Soldiers going off to war left shortages of skilled workers at home. This triggered a huge demand for training, especially in technical subjects. Community colleges increased their two-year degree programs and grew into trade schools. Schools and colleges were put under further strain when teachers decided to leave the profession for better-paying work elsewhere. It is estimated that between 1939 and 1944 more than one hundred thousand teachers took jobs in the defense industries or in the military. In 1946, seventy-five thousand American children went without schooling because of teacher shortages. Desperate education committees hired poor-quality teachers to fill the gaps.

The universities gained more from the war than did the public schools. The federal government funded specialized war-related research, which boosted university revenues. The Massachusetts Institute of Technology (MIT), for example, received $117 million for radar research. The success of such projects convinced educators like Vannevar Bush that the federal government and the nation's universities also should work together after the war. More challenging for higher education was the Servicemen's Readjustment Act, passed by Congress on June 22, 1944. Known as the GI Bill, the act paid college fees for soldiers reentering civilian life after the war. In all, 7.8 million veterans packed college classrooms. The enrollment surge put a huge strain on colleges, but it meant that millions of Americans received a college education. Many of these students were the first members of their families to graduate from college.

After the war, American educators were divided into two groups. Conservatives argued for religious education in schools, for separate facilities for black and white students, and for local funding for schools. Progressives wanted a national, standardized school system. They argued that the war had shown the need for education in politics and economics. Progressives were also often, though not always, in favor of mixed-race schools. Conservative educators lost support during the 1940s. A Supreme Court decision, *McCollum* v. *Board of Education,* ruled that religious instruction in public schools was unconstitutional. The National Association for the Advancement of Colored People (NAACP) won a series of small legal victories during the decade that would lead to mixed-race schooling in the 1950s. Many people agreed with progressive educators that the United States needed a national education system.

Besides rebuilding education at home, American educators were also working hard abroad. The United Nations Educational, Scientific, and Cultural Organization (UNESCO) was established to improve understanding between nations, to fund libraries and museums, and to encourage research. By 1945, universities such as Columbia, Stanford, Princeton, and Yale had opened schools of international relations. New institutes were set up to study the cultures of other countries such as Russia, Germany, and France. American colleges were opened in Florence, Italy; Biarritz, France; and Shrivenham, England. American educators also helped rebuild the German and Japanese education systems. By the end of the 1940s, American educators had considerable cultural influence around the world.

Mortimer Adler (1902–2001) Mortimer Adler was a promoter of the "Great Books" project of the 1940s. He believed that by studying the great works of literature, philosophy, and science, students could learn all they needed to know about Western culture. A compulsive man who liked to keep everything tidy and in order, Adler had a temperament that was perfect for the project. He spent many years perfecting his list of "Great Books." Though the Great Books project never really caught on in colleges, Adler became a household name through sales of his own books.

Photo reproduced by permission of AP/Wide World Photos.

Sarah G. Blanding (1898–1985) In 1937, Sarah G. Blanding became an assistant professor of political science at the University of Kentucky, where she was also dean of women. After a career at Cornell University, she became president of Vassar College in 1946. She was an adviser to the federal government on women in higher education, and led army and navy committees on welfare and recreation for women. For her work she was given the War Department's Civilian Service Award in 1946. *Photo courtesy of the Library of Congress.*

Andrew David Holt (1904–1972) Andrew David Holt took control of the nation's biggest teachers union, the National Education Association (NEA), in 1949. He completed his Ph.D. at Columbia University in 1937 and spent several years campaigning for better pay, sick leave, and retirement pay for teachers. During wartime service in the U.S. Army, Holt traveled the country lecturing students and faculty on how to help the war effort. After his election in 1949, the NEA voted to purge communists from its membership in a resolution called the "Preservation of Democracy." Although it argued for freedom in the classroom, the resolution was actually an attack on free speech.

Robert M. Hutchins (1899–1977) By the age of thirty, Robert M. Hutchins had become president of the University of Chicago, a post he held from 1927 to 1945. He made dramatic changes in the way the university was run and the courses it offered. Many of his reforms have become standard practice in higher education. Hutchins allowed students many more freedoms than before. They could choose their own courses from a set of electives, and they were allowed to attend dances and go on dates. He is famous for promoting the idea that a good education involved reading the "Great Books" of Western culture. In the 1950s, Hutchins defended his faculty against anticommunist investigators, and he fought for free speech throughout his life. *Photo reproduced by permission of the Corbis Corporation.*

Owen Lattimore (1900–1989) As one of the foremost experts on Asia, Owen Lattimore became a political adviser to Chiang Kai-Sheck of China in 1941. Throughout World War II (1939–45) he also advised the U.S. federal government on Asian affairs. After the war he returned to teaching in the United States, but in the 1950s Lattimore was accused of being a communist sympathizer and spy. The case was dropped. Yet despite writing three acclaimed books on Japan and Asia, and despite his contribution to American education, Lattimore's academic career was ruined. Few students would risk their own careers to work with him because of the communist charges. *Photo reproduced by permission of the Corbis Corporation.*

Frederick Douglas Patterson (1901–1988) In 1943, Frederick Douglas Patterson created the United Negro College Fund (UNCF) to help African Americans attend and graduate from college. As president of Tuskegee Normal and Industrial Institute, Patterson was a key figure in the introduction of the federal school lunch program. He believed that good nutrition was essential to educational achievement. In 1947, he served on President Truman's Commission on Higher Education, recommending more grants and scholarships and an end to separate education for whites and blacks. *Photo reproduced by permission of the Frederick D. Patterson Research Institute.*

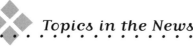

Topics in the News

❖ TEACHERS AND PROFESSORS RESIST POLITICAL PRESSURE

The principle of academic freedom is that university teachers should be able to teach and research any subject that will benefit students and society as a whole. In the 1940s, conservative politicians and church leaders made many attacks on academic freedom. Some university teachers were accused of trying to turn their students into communists. Others were challenged for their ideas about marriage, sex, and religion.

The most famous academic freedom dispute of the decade is the Bertrand Russell case. Russell (1872–1970) was one of the twentieth century's most brilliant philosophers. He was hired to teach logic and mathematics at New York City College in 1940. But conservatives were alarmed by Russell's unconventional views on marriage and sexuality. The philosopher was also a prominent left-wing thinker. Newspapers described him as an "anarchist" (someone who prefers to do away with all forms of government), while clergy disliked the fact that he did not believe in God and was hostile to organized religion. Soon after Russell's hiring, and before he entered the classroom, the New York courts ruled against his appointment. One of the reasons given was that Russell was "unqualified" to teach at City College. But since Russell was one of the world's greatest philosophers and an acclaimed mathematician, there was nobody better qualified to do so.

Any hope of an appeal faded when Mayor Fiorello La Guardia (1882–1947) withdrew funding for Russell's post at City College. The Russell case damaged academic freedom because it denied the right of academics to judge the quality of the work of their colleagues. Instead, a politician had decided whom City College could employ. American philosopher and educator John Dewey (1859–1952) was a vocal opponent of Russell's views. But even Dewey thought the case was a national embarrassment. He said: "We can only blush with shame for this scar on our repute for fair play." Politicians were not the only ones who tried to limit academic freedoms; they were joined by education administrators. At the University of Chicago, in 1944, president Robert M. Hutchins (1899–1977) tried to abolish academic rank, effectively reducing senior professors to the level of junior colleagues. When news of his effort appeared in the national press, the plan was dropped.

In primary and secondary schools the situation was similar. Throughout the 1940s, teachers known to be communists were suspected of brainwashing their students. In fact, there was no evidence that communist teachers were better or worse at their job than anyone else. But conservative adminis-trators and school board officials often damaged the reputation of left-wing teachers by labeling them as "Reds." Schools themselves often were investi-gated for evidence of communist or fascist views. The New York Assembly appointed the Rapp-Condert Committee in 1941 to seek out fascists (people who supported governments run by dictators such as Germany's Adolf Hitler). They soon turned to hunting "Reds," and twenty-five instructors were fired for their left-wing views. Yet the committee could find no evidence that the fired teachers had been instructing their students in communism or fascism.

The most powerful threat to teachers came from the federal government in the form of the House Un-American Activities Committee (HUAC), a committee formed by the U.S. House of Representatives. In 1949, HUAC began inspecting textbooks for signs of communist material. The same year, the National Education Association (NEA) voted to ban members who were known to be communists. School boards also began forcing teachers to swear an oath that they were not members of the Communist Party.

In the universities, anticommunist fervor was slower to arrive. Still, in 1947, Harvard Uni-versity came under attack. Many of its faculty were outspoken liberals. They supported Henry Wallace (1888–1965) in his run for president of the United States on a Progressive Party ticket. The high standing of Harvard and its faculty pro-tected them from real threat, but elsewhere pro-fessors had more trouble. At the University of Washington, several faculty members were expelled for refusing to cooperate with an inves-tigation. Both Oklahoma and California began forcing teachers and college faculty to sign loyalty oaths in 1949. Thirty-one professors were fired for refusing to sign. But though careers were ruined, far worse was the effect on American universities. Attacks on academic freedom made them less dynamic, less outspoken, and less interesting as places to work and study.

Philosopher Bertrand Russell, one of the most important American philosophers of the twentieth century, was declared "unqualified" to teach at New York City College because of his controversial views on marriage, sexuality, and other hot topics. **Courtesy of the Library of Congress.**

❖ AMERICAN EDUCATION PROMOTES INTERNATIONAL UNDERSTANDING

In November 1945, representatives of forty-four countries met in Lon-don to adopt the constitution of the United Nations Educational, Scientific, and Cultural Organization (UNESCO). Even before 1945, UNESCO's founders had used their influence to prevent the bombing of university cities such as Oxford England, and Heidelberg Germany. In 1946, UNESCO became an agency of the United Nations (UN). It funded the rebuilding of 362 libraries around Europe, 4 museums in Belgium, 1,326 churches in Yugoslavia, and many other institutions damaged or destroyed by bombs.

UNESCO was helped greatly by the U.S. occupation of European countries and Japan. Apart from rebuilding libraries and museums, UNESCO was also involved in restoring schooling to children in war-torn countries. Under the Marshall Plan (a program that used American money to rebuild the economies of Europe and Asia), the U.S. Army employed teachers, scientists, and students to help teach about world peace. In both Germany and Japan, UNESCO helped undo the effects of years of fascist propaganda. UNESCO aimed to encourage human rights, promote the arts around the world, and improve living conditions worldwide. When the cold war began in 1947, however, most UNESCO peacekeeping programs came to an end.

Perhaps the most important American program to promote international understanding was the Fulbright-Hays Act. Senator James W. Fulbright (1905–1995) of Arkansas put Public Law 584 before Congress in 1946, where it was passed in August of that year. The act paid for academics and students to study abroad. These "Fulbright Scholars" would gain knowledge and understanding of other cultures while promoting American culture abroad. Fulbright scholarships were a great success, soon ranking among the most prestigious academic awards. By the mid-1990s, twelve thousand American students had traveled to other countries on Fulbright scholarships, and fifteen thousand students from abroad had studied in the United States.

❖ A CURRICULUM WITH CULTURE AT ITS CORE

World War II exposed severe problems with the American public school system. Children from different parts of the country had widely different experiences of schooling. After the war ended, education specialists began to debate ways of reforming the secondary and postsecondary curriculum. Led by University of Chicago president Robert M. Hutchins (1899–1977), they proposed what they called a "core curriculum." This was a curriculum focused on the arts, humanities, and "Great Books." The aim was to insure that all secondary-school students had a grounding in what Hutchins called the "tradition of the West."

The ideas behind the core curriculum went against many of the education reforms of the 1930s. Before the war, American education had con-

In 1937, Stringfellow Barr (1897–1982) became president of St. John's College in Annapolis, Maryland. He was a close associate of Robert M. Hutchins at the University of Chicago, and a supporter of the core curriculum. He was also an advisory editor for Encyclopedia Britannica's Great Books series. At St. John's in the 1940s, Barr organized a course of study based on one hundred great books and began teaching it to the college's 231 male students. Barr left St. John's in 1946, fearing it had grown too large, but the first graduates of the system completed their studies in 1949. Barr's idea did not catch on elsewhere. Still, in the twenty-first century St. John's College continues to base its entire curriculum on the study of "Great Books" ranging from the *Bible* through the *Constitution of the United States* to Richard Wagner's opera *Tristan and Isolde*.

centrated on the sciences, economics, and psychology. Literature, the arts, and other humanities also had their place, but students specialized early and thus lacked general knowledge of Western culture. Hutchins argued that such a narrow education created citizens who were materialistic and lacking in moral values. The core curriculum was intended to rescue American culture from its obsession with money.

After the war ended, the core curriculum project began to take shape. Clifton Fadiman (1904–1999), Mark van Doren (1894–1972), Jacques Barzun (1907–), and others pressed Hutchins to introduce the core curriculum at the University of Chicago. Philosopher Mortimer Adler (1902–2001) proposed a course of "Great Books" where students would read a "classic a week" from the fields of literature, philosophy, theology, and political theory. Hutchins suggested a two-year core curriculum at the University of Chicago, followed by specialized graduate study. Although the two-year course was never offered, the "Great Books" idea did influence university and college courses at Chicago and around the country.

Although the core curriculum was never adopted nationally, the idea of a "core" of Great Books that could improve American society was very attractive. Many educators used the concept to design courses in schools, colleges, and universities. Hutchins and his supporters produced many books on the subject among them are Van Doren's *Liberal Education*

(1943) and Hutchins' own *Education for Freedom* (1943). They argued that the rise of fascism and communism could be blamed on a lack of education in the humanities.

They also attacked progressive educators who argued for a specialized curriculum, which was the opposite of the Great Books concept. Adler attacked progressive John Dewey, arguing that democracy had more to fear from experimenters like him than from fascists like Hitler. Adler's attack came in 1940, when the German army was preparing to overrun Europe. It was an insensitive remark, which shocked many people, but it also succeeded in damaging the progressive cause. A few years later, progressives were no longer accused of being right-wing fascists. Instead, they were attacked as left-wing communists.

But while attacks on progressives were successful, the core curriculum idea itself did not gain ground. The main problem was in trying to decide which books should be listed as "classics." Even supporters of the idea could not agree. Adler argued that a classic was a work that had "stood the test of time" and offered insight into human nature. He produced a list of titles that met his requirements. Critics were not convinced. They doubted whether many of the books on the list did have universal value, and wondered instead if the works had value only for people like Adler. This was the main problem with the Great Books concept. Critics charged that it tried to force the views of wealthy, educated white people onto students from all social and ethnic backgrounds.

Because of the influence of the "Great Books" program on colleges nationwide, publishers such as the Encyclopedia Britannica produced many "Great Books" sets.
Reproduced by permission of Getty Images, Inc.

❖ THE FEDERAL GOVERNMENT BUYS LUNCH IN SCHOOLS

Until the 1930s, American schools had always been funded locally. During the Great Depression, the Roosevelt administration helped out local school boards with federal aid. At the end of World War II, the U.S. government began a program to expand education. It sold off 100,000 acres of land and 2,500 buildings at just 3.5 percent of their market value. In doing so it helped establish 5,500 public schools, colleges, and universities. Yet, by the end of the 1940s, there was still no regular system of federal assistance for education.

For women, the 1940s brought improved access to education. Wartime labor shortages meant that many women left school early to go to work. This forced colleges to create courses that would keep them in school. In the 1920s, women had been taught to run a home and look after children. In the 1940s, they became lawyers, chemists, and engineers. But even though women were encouraged to stay in college, men and women still were educated separately. In 1947, Harvard University allowed female students from nearby Radcliffe College to attend classes with men. Radcliffe became the first Ivy League coeducational school. Most colleges, universities, and state-supported schools followed Harvard's lead within a few years.

The idea of federal funding for education was highly controversial. Congress repeatedly rejected funding bills after the war. Conservatives and liberals alike opposed federal funding. Conservatives feared that it would mean the spread of progressive education (an educational approach that favored student participation rather than learning by rote). In the South, conservatives worried that federal funding would end segregation and lead to blacks and whites being educated together. Liberals opposed federal funding for other reasons. They saw it as a way for federal government to take control of the curriculum and dominate teachers. Though federal funding plans were often supported by President Truman, schools remained under local control.

Despite the opposition, in certain areas federal funding was a success in the 1940s. When the war ended, hundreds of thousands of veterans had to be helped back into society. The government opened military schools that offered a nonmilitary education. The United States Armed Forces Institute offered 275 courses in 1944. By February 1946, eight hundred thousand veterans were taking correspondence courses. But the most popular innovation of all was the school lunch program. In 1940, the federal government paid $2 million to buy meals for elementary and secondary school students; by 1949, the figure had risen to $92 million. Though he was usually a strong critic of the Democrats, even former President Herbert Hoover (1874–1964) was enthusiastic about the school lunch program, which had been started by a Democratic presidential administration.

❖ VETERANS GO BACK TO SCHOOL

The Servicemen's Readjustment Act (GI Bill of Rights) has gone down in history as one of the most forward-looking pieces of legislation ever passed by the U.S. Congress. The reasons for establishing the GI Bill were simple. Veterans of World War II deserved to be compensated for the sacrifices they had made in defending democracy. It was also important that they should settle back into civilian life. The U.S. economy would have to absorb around sixteen million veterans of the European and Pacific campaigns. In order to make sure the transition from war to peace went smoothly, Congress passed the GI Bill in 1944, and President Franklin D. Roosevelt signed it into law that year.

The GI Bill allowed any veteran who had served ninety or more days after September 16, 1940, to receive up to two years of education or training at the government's expense. The Veterans' Administration paid school costs of up to $500 each year, and also gave each GI a monthly payment to cover living expenses. In 1945, veterans in college received $65 per month if they were single and $90 if they had dependents. Just over half of the eligible veterans joined the program. Up to 1947, when it closed, the GI Bill cost $14.5 billion.

With so much government money available, the GI Bill was easily abused. American colleges and universities set new enrollment records in 1947 and raised their fees to record levels. Between 1939 and 1947, the cost to attend law school rose by 46 percent. Fees had also shot up elsewhere, by 27 percent at private schools, and by 29 percent at public schools. There were warnings that when government money stopped flowing, colleges and universities would have to reduce their tuition.

Another problem caused by the GI Bill was overcrowding. Many educational institutions simply could not handle so many new students. There were shortages of classrooms, professors, and books. New programs and night classes were begun to ease the pressure. Junior colleges and community colleges expanded to deal with the extra students. Veterans who needed high school credits were given special classes so they did not have to attend regular high school with teenagers. They worked from condensed texts, and teachers were trained to move them through the material as quickly as possible.

Eventually, problems with the GI Bill forced a Select Committee investigation into alleged abuses. But despite the difficulties, the GI Bill was a huge success for veterans who took advantage of the offer. Veterans who were better educated landed better paying jobs. The GI Bill gave many people an opportunity for personal development they would not

Soldiers who could not read or write were called "jugheads" by their fellow GIs. In 1945, there were more than three hundred thousand jugheads in the U.S. Army. But the army was very good at teaching basic reading and writing skills. It boasted that its system of flash cards, movies, and word recognition could teach soldiers to read and write in just eight weeks. The system certainly worked, but education specialists realized it would be difficult to use it in ordinary schools. Unlike normal students, soldiers could be forced to study at any time of the day or night. They were also desperate to be able to read letters from their loved ones and to write replies home.

otherwise have had. It helped expand the American middle class in the postwar period.

❖ AMERICAN HIGH SCHOOLS NOT UP TO SCRATCH

In November 1946, high school students in Rogersville, Tennessee, went on strike to demand better-quality teachers. They asked the school principal to find teachers with at least four years of college training and five years of teaching experience. Teachers also had to be willing to work for $149 per month at a time when the cheapest new car cost around $1,200. It was almost impossible. Anyone clever enough to be a teacher could earn considerably more money doing something else. Many schools closed because there were not enough teachers to work in them. Teachers who did stay in the classroom often went on strike over low pay in the 1940s.

Strikes, shortages of teachers, and closures were not the only problems facing American high schools in the 1940s. The whole system was badly organized, badly run, and close to chaos. By law in every state, children had to attend school until the age of sixteen, but thousands of children had no school to go to. The quality and type of education varied from one town to the next. World War II exposed the poor state of American schooling. Millions of young men were refused entry to the military because they could not read. The Naval Officers' Training Corps reported that sixty-two out of every one hundred candidates failed the simple arithmetic test.

The sorry state of U.S. public education negatively affected more than just the military. While many students dropped out of school to enlist in the military, many more left to find work. These dropouts found themselves with little education and no adult supervision. Many of them spent

their days working in dull, dead-end jobs and their nights causing trouble. By the end of the war, only seven out of every ten high school students went as far as grades eleven and twelve. U.S. Commissioner of Education John W. Studebaker (1887–1989) decided to change the curriculum to encourage teenagers to stay in school.

The "Lifestyle Adjustment Curriculum," as it was called, was based on the assumption that 60 percent of high school students either were not smart enough to go to college, or were not technically minded enough to benefit from technical training. The curriculum aimed to give these 60 percent the skills they would need to have a happy life and make a useful contribution to society. They would study applied business math instead of more advanced mathematics. Communication skills would replace "hard" subjects such as literature and grammar. Because it was less daunting, the Lifestyle Adjustment Curriculum was thought to be able to keep students in school. From 1945 onwards, it began to spread slowly across the country.

There were many critics of the less challenging curriculum. Some thought it would lead high schools to abandon their "true purpose" of providing intellectual training. Historian Richard Hofstadter (1916–1970) actually saw danger in the Lifestyle Adjustment Curriculum. He argued that it was not intended to help students achieve their potential. Rather, it molded them into easily managed, passive citizens who would not give the government any trouble. Criticism of the curriculum prevented it from being widely adopted, and by the end of the decade little had changed in most high schools. By the 1950s, the ineffectiveness of American education threatened to weaken the country's standing as a world power.

❖ EDUCATION MOVES TOWARD RACIAL EQUALITY

In the 1940s, black and white children went to separate schools in the South, where segregation was enforced by law. It was part of a system known as Jim Crow laws. In theory, Jim Crow laws gave "separate but equal" treatment to blacks and whites. The reality was rather different. In 1949, for example, Clarendon County, South Carolina, spent $179 each year on every white child enrolled in school. The county spent only $43 for each black child. As a result, schools for African Americans were usually in a terrible condition. They were overcrowded and unheated. In winter, children often wore their overcoats to keep warm in the classroom. Some white children also suffered similar hardship. But for blacks, it was common. This unequal treatment violated the Fourteenth Amendment to the U.S. Constitution. But as long as school boards appeared to be doing what they could to act fairly, the courts took no notice.

OPPOSITE PAGE
G. W. McLaurin was the one of the first African American students accepted at the University of Oklahoma. Because of discriminatory policies, he was forced to attend classes by himself in a classroom separate from white students.
Reproduced by permission of the Corbis Corporation.

Religious Education

The 1940s saw the end of compulsory religious education in American public schools. When Vashti McCollum refused to allow her son Terry to attend religious classes, she ended up before the U.S. Supreme Court. In *McCollum v. Board of Education,* she argued that classes in religion were unfair to minority religious faiths, and that church and state should be separate. The court ruled in her favor. After an appeal in 1948, the Supreme Court found that religious instruction or activity in public schools was unconstitutional. Religious discussion was not forbidden, but it had to be part of an effort to create responsible citizens of all beliefs.

The National Association for the Advancement of Colored People (NAACP) had been fighting racial equality cases throughout the 1930s. In the 1940s it finally began to make progress. Major industries such as defense equipment plants were desegregated, so blacks and whites began working together. In 1948, President Truman desegregated the military. Father Joseph E. Ritter (1882–1967) of St. Louis, Missouri, succeeded in desegregating Catholic schools and in 1948, New Jersey desegregated its schools. By then, several colleges, including the Universities of Maryland and Arkansas, had begun admitting African Americans. The following year, Wesley A. Brown (1927–) became the first black graduate from the U.S. Naval Academy to receive a commission as an officer. But there were still obstacles. A 1949 attempt to desegregate schools in Washington, D.C., failed. Even so, by the end of the decade, Jim Crow laws were starting to fall apart.

The main reason separate education for blacks and whites could not last was money. As the NAACP put pressure on school boards to improve education for black students, it became clear that the costs to maintain segregation would be huge. In 1948, the Board of Control for Southern Regional Education began discussing the possibility of creating separate but truly equal facilities for blacks and whites. In 1949, they revealed that the cost of raising the standard of black school facilities to the same level as for whites would be $545 million. Jim Crow laws were absurdly expensive. In the universities, the situation was similar. The University of Oklahoma Law School created a separate facility for just three black students. Elsewhere, black students were separated from their white counterparts by sheets, which divided the classroom. A court in Oklahoma finally came to the conclusion that "separate education is inherently unequal."

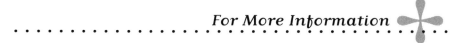

For More Information

BOOKS

Bernard, Sheila Curran, and Sarah Mondale, eds. *School: The Story of American Public Education*. Boston: Beacon Press, 2001.

Calvi, Gian. *How UNESCO Sees a World for Everybody*. Paris: UNESCO, 1979.

Dorman, Michael. *Witch Hunt: The Underside of American Democracy*. New York: Delacorte Press, 1976.

Duden, Jane. *1940s*. New York: Crestwood House, 1989.

Eaton, William Edward. *The American Federation of Teachers, 1916–1961: A History of the Movement*. Carbondale, IL: Southern Illinois University Press, 1975.

Feinstein, Stephen. *The 1940s from World War II to Jackie Robinson*. Berkeley Heights, NJ: Enslow Publishers, 2000.

Foner, Eric, and John A. Garraty, eds. *The Reader's Companion to American History*. New York: Houghton Mifflin, 1991.

Hills, Ken. *1940s*. Austin, TX: Raintree Steck-Vaughn, 1992.

Isaacs, Sally Senzell. *America in the Time of Franklin Delano Roosevelt: The Story of Our Nation from Coast to Coast, from 1929 to 1948*. Des Plaines, IL: Heinemann Library, 2000.

Lee, Winifred Trask. *A Forest of Pencils: The Story of Schools Through the Ages*. Indianapolis: Bobbs-Merrill, 1973.

Matthews, Rupert. *Going to School*. New York: Franklin Watts, 2000.

Press, Petra. *A Multicultural Portrait of Learning in America*. New York: Marshall Cavendish, 1994.

Pulliam, John D. *History of Education in America*. Columbus, OH: Merrill, 1982.

Reef, Catherine. *Childhood in America*. New York: Facts on File, 2002.

Seely, Gordon M. *Education and Opportunity: For What and For Whom?* Englewood Cliffs, NJ: Prentice-Hall, 1977.

Spring, Joel. *The American School: 1642–1985*. New York: Longman, 1986.

Trotter, Joe William. *From a Raw Deal to a New Deal?: African Americans, 1929–1945*. New York: Oxford University Press, 1996.

Uschan, Michael V. *The 1940s*. San Diego, CA: Lucent Books, 1999.

Wiedlich, Thom. *Appointment Denied: The Inquisition of Bertrand Russell*. Amherst, NY: Prometheus Books, 2000.

PERIODICALS

"The 101 Great Ideas." *Life* (January 26, 1948): pp. 92-102.

WEB SITES

The History of Education and Childhood. [Online] http://www.socsci.kun.nl/ped/whp/histeduc/index.html (accessed March 2002).

St. John's College: Where Great Books Are the Teachers. [Online] http://www.sjca.edu (accessed March, 2002).

chapter four *Government, Politics, and Law*

1940: June 10 President Franklin D. Roosevelt declares that the American stance on the war in Europe is changing from "neutrality" to "nonbelligerency."

1940: June 28 The Smith Act makes it illegal to demand the overthrow of the United States government by force or to found any group with that aim.

1940: November 5 Roosevelt is reelected president by an electoral college landslide.

1940: December 29 Roosevelt makes his "arsenal of democracy" speech, promising to supply the Allies with munitions.

1941: October 30 The USS *Reuben James* is sunk in the Atlantic by a German submarine. Although one hundred sailors lost their lives in the attack, the American public still wants to stay out of the war.

1941: December 7 Japanese planes bomb the American military base in Pearl Harbor, Hawaii. Public opinion swings instantly in favor of entering the war.

1941: December 22 A new military draft act requires all males aged eighteen to sixty-five to register for military service. Those between twenty and forty-four had to be prepared to be called up for active duty.

1942: January 1 The Declaration of the United Nations is signed, with the United States as one of twenty-six signatories.

1942: January 12 The National War Labor Board is set up to settle labor disputes.

1942: February 19 President Roosevelt signs an executive order excluding selected persons from areas along the west coast of the United States. By March 29, over 110,000 Japanese Americans have been moved to internment camps away from the coast.

1942: June 4–6 After the Battle of Midway in the Pacific, the Japanese advance is halted.

1942: November 8 Operation Torch moves 400,000 Allied troops onto the beaches of North Africa.

1943: June 10 The Current Tax Payment Act takes effect. For the first time, Americans have taxes deducted from their paychecks.

1943: November 28 The leaders of the United States, Britain, and the Soviet Union meet in Tehran, Iran, to plan the Allied invasion of Europe.

1944: April 3 In *Smith* v. *Allwright,* the U.S. Supreme Court rules that blacks cannot be denied the right to vote in the Texas Democratic primary.

1944: July 21 Roosevelt becomes the first person to be nominated for a fourth term as president of the United States.

1945: American forces take back territories in the Pacific captured by the Japanese. These include the Philippines and the islands of Iwo Jima and Okinawa. There are many thousands of casualties on both sides.

1945: **February 11** At the Yalta conference, the three main Allied powers agree on the postwar division of Europe.

1945: **April 12** Roosevelt dies of a cerebral hemorrhage. Vice President Harry S Truman is sworn in as president.

1945: **April 30** Nazi leader Adolf Hitler kills himself in Berlin.

1945: **May 8** Germany surrenders, ending the European phase of the war. Victory in Europe (V-E) Day is declared.

1945: **August 6** The Japanese city of Hiroshima is destroyed by an atomic bomb dropped by the United States. The destruction stuns even the scientists who invented the bomb. Three days later, a second bomb is dropped on Nagasaki, Japan.

1945: **September 2** Japan surrenders. Victory in Japan (V-J) Day is declared.

1945: **November 12** War-crime trials of Nazis begin in Nuremburg, Germany.

1946: The segregation of blacks and whites on interstate buses is declared unconstitutional.

1946: Tensions between the United States and the Soviet Union rise as the Soviets work to create their own atomic bomb to restore the balance of military power between the two countries.

1947: **March 12** President Truman announces his "containment" policy, which is designed to stop the expansion of the Soviet Union. Truman also provides $400 million to Greece and Turkey to fight the spread of Communism.

1947: **July 18** The Presidential Succession Act makes the Speaker of the House of Representatives next in line for the presidency after the vice president.

1947: **October 29** President Truman calls for an end to segregation and equal rights for all races.

1948: Both the Democrats and the Republicans ask World War II hero General Dwight D. Eisenhower to run for president.

1948: **June 25** The Displaced Persons Act allows more than two hundred thousand refugees from Eastern Europe to enter the United States.

1948: **November 2** Defying the polls, President Truman is reelected.

1949: **January 19** Congress raises the president's salary to $100,000 per year. He is allowed $50,000 in expenses.

1949: **April 4** The North Atlantic Treaty Organization (NATO) is founded as a defense pact among the Western Allies.

Overview

The United States emerged as a world leader during the 1940s. President Franklin D. Roosevelt knew that World War II (1939–45) would bring an end to the British Empire and reduce British influence. He managed America's involvement in the war so that the United States could replace Britain in world affairs after 1945. Roosevelt led America through the war with a minimum number of casualties. But after his death, critics blamed him for the survival of the Soviet Union and the beginning of the cold war.

The war affected almost every aspect of American life. It ended the Great Depression (1930–39), provided work for everyone, and raised incomes. By the end of the decade, the United States had a large and well-off middle class. Giant corporations had begun to dominate American business, while the federal government had immense wealth and power. All of these changes had an effect on the operation of American government and the law. But the most dramatic change in American political life was the rising power of the military.

Before 1939, the United States had no tradition of a large, professional army. World War II brought sixteen million Americans into military service. After the war, the government operated under the assumption that the country was under threat from the Soviet Union and other Communist nations. It therefore established the Department of Defense, the Central Intelligence Agency (CIA), and the National Security Council in the 1940s to combat this threat. The government formed alliances with weapons manufacturers to create what became known as the "military-industrial complex," a term that describes how the government, business, and major universities worked together to support military buildup. After 1945, Americans became suspicious of those countries that did not share their aims or beliefs, and they armed themselves for defense.

Before the Japanese bombing of Pearl Harbor on December 7, 1941, most Americans were against entering the war. Even after the Japanese attack, public opinion had to be managed carefully. President Roosevelt and his advisers knew that if American casualties rose too high, the policy of total defeat for the Germans and the Japanese might fail. The federal government concentrated on armaments manufacturing. And though around eight million Americans saw combat, America's three hundred thousand casualties were small compared with those suffered by other nations. Russia, for example, lost twenty-five million citizens in the fight with Nazi Germany. Roosevelt knew the limits of his support and he stayed within them.

In the 1930s, Americans had come to appreciate the economic security that President Roosevelt's "New Deal" policies had given them. Even Republicans such as Wendell Willkie and Thomas E. Dewey argued in favor of the welfare state set up by the Democrats. They split away from conservatives in their own party. But in the strange political climate of the postwar years, the Republican right wing gained power again. Senator Joseph McCarthy and House member Richard Nixon attacked the Truman administration for not doing enough to guard against Communism. McCarthy's supporters tapped into a public mood of distrust and suspicion toward foreigners and liberals. Their methods of intimidation and accusation would raise many questions about the safety of American democracy and justice.

Although in some ways Americans became more distrustful after 1945, in other ways the war made them more open and tolerant. The death camps in Germany led to tribunals, which brought war criminals to justice. The terrible treatment of Jews, Gypsies, and other prisoners captured by the Germans and Japanese increased Americans' willingness to consider the civil rights of African Americans. The United States ended the decade with a reorganized government and a more powerful military. The American legal system, led by the Supreme Court, would have to find a balance between an increasingly open society and those who thought that such openness was dangerous.

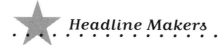

Thomas E. Dewey (1902–1971) On the day after the 1948 presidential election, President Harry S Truman was photographed holding the first edition of the *Chicago Daily Tribune*. Its banner headline declared a Thomas Dewey victory! In fact, Truman won by 2.2 million popular votes and 144 electoral votes. But despite his defeats in two presidential elections, Dewey had a long and successful political career. As governor of New York, he had a reputation for being hard on gangsters, and in the 1940s Dewey became popular for reducing taxes. He *Photo courtesy of the Library of Congress.*

Dwight D. Eisenhower (1890–1969) In 1938, Dwight D. Eisenhower was thinking of retiring from the army. But World War II gave him the opportunity to reach the highest levels in the U.S. military and government. He led Operation Torch, the invasion of North Africa in November 1941, and he went on to lead Operation Overlord on June 6, 1944, commonly known as D-Day. During this battle, Eisenhower successfully coordinated 2.8 million personnel and landed thousands of Allied troops on the beaches in Normandy, France. In 1950, he took command of the North Atlantic Treaty Organization (NATO). He was elected president of the United States in 1952, holding the office until 1960. *Photo courtesy of the National Archives and Records Administration.*

Alger Hiss (1904–1996) In 1948, Whittaker Chambers, a magazine editor and former Communist Party courier, accused high government official Alger Hiss of having helped transmit confidential government documents to the Russians. When Hiss was first brought to trial in 1949, the jury was unable to reach a decision. At a second trial Hiss was found guilty and sentenced to a five-year prison term. He was released from prison in 1954. In 1957, he wrote *In the Court of Public Opinion*, in which he denied all charges against him. Hiss maintained his innocence to his death; Soviet files made public in 1995 convinced most observers that he had been guilty, but controversy lingers. *Photo courtesy of the Library of Congress.*

Charles Houston (1895–1950) Charles Houston was one of the major civil rights leaders of the twentieth century. He paved the way for later more famous figures such as Martin Luther King Jr. (1929–1968) and Thurgood Marshall (1908–1993). Houston enrolled in Harvard Law School in 1919, graduating in 1922. Between 1935 and 1940 he was special counsel to the National Association for the Advancement of Colored People (NAACP), and later served as chairman of the group's legal committee until shortly before his death in 1950. *Photo reproduced by permission of the Corbis Corporation.*

George C. Marshall (1880–1959) George C. Marshall managed American military strategy during World War II and later became one of the main strategists of the cold war. His "Marshall Plan" helped reconstruct Europe in the late 1940s, and in 1953 he became the only soldier ever to win the Nobel Peace Prize. But while the Marshall Plan and his diplomatic missions to China in 1945 certainly helped restore peace to the world, Marshall was criticized for his part in the decision to drop atomic bombs on Japan.

Frances Perkins (1882–1965) Frances Perkins was the first woman ever appointed to a cabinet position in the U.S. government. From 1933 onwards, she helped reshape the labor market and bring new rights, better pay, and safer working conditions to millions of Americans. But because of her views on unemployment assistance, as well as her attacks on private industry, she was labeled a communist. In 1939, the Republicans began impeachment proceedings against her, but they were dropped. She served in the U.S. Civil Service Commission from 1945 to 1953. *Photo reproduced by permission of AP/Wide World Photos.*

Franklin D. Roosevelt (1882–1945) Franklin D. Roosevelt is the only person to have been elected to the U.S. presidency four times. Over that period he became one of the most respected and best-loved of all presidents. He saw the United States through the Great Depression and most of World War II. Conservatives often criticized Roosevelt for imposing limits on business and for championing the rights of ordinary people. His critics also thought he was devious and dictatorial. But Roosevelt made the country the wealthiest and most powerful in the world. *Photo reproduced by permission of the Corbis Corporation.*

Harry S Truman (1884–1972) Harry S Truman became president when President Franklin D. Roosevelt died in April 1945. He was committed to fairness and justice at home and abroad, but one of his first acts as president was deciding to drop atomic bombs on Japan. He also became well known for the "Truman Doctrine," which promised to fund anticommunists in Europe. Truman was a champion of civil rights, helping to bring about the end of the racist Jim Crow system in the South. His obituary in the *New York Times* ran for seven pages. *Photo reproduced by permission of AP/Wide World Photos.*

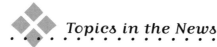

Topics in the News

❖ THE UNITED STATES JOINS THE WAR

At the end of World War I (1914–18), Germany was punished by the victorious Allies (led by France, Great Britain, and the United States). In the Treaty of Versailles, which ended World War I, Germany was forced to surrender territory and to admit to having started the war. Of the Allies, only the United States wanted Germany returned to full strength. With their national pride wounded, by 1933 Germans were ready to elect as their leader the fascist Adolf Hitler (1889–1945). He promised to restore the country's dignity. In the late 1930s, Germany, Italy, and Japan (known as the Axis powers) were planning to build empires in Europe, East Asia, and Africa. With American economic interests under threat, by 1940 many American officials thought war would be the only way to achieve peace.

The war in Europe began on September 3, 1939, when Hitler's armies invaded Poland. But even after fighting had begun, Americans were reluctant to get involved. The public believed that the United States had been pushed into World War I by bankers and arms manufacturers seeking to make a profit. Those who did not want to see this happen again were known as isolationists. They believed that the United States should stay isolated from problems abroad.

Isolationists such as the famous aviator Charles Lindbergh (1902– 1974) wanted to create "Fortress America," keeping the United States safe from the corrupting influence of Europe. Their opponents, known as interventionists, thought that the only way to protect American interests was to be active abroad. This did not always mean direct military action. Many interventionists felt that America could help defeat fascism by supplying nations such as Great Britain with ships, airplanes, and tanks. Other Americans saw military action as the only way to save democracy from the fascist governments in Germany, Italy, and Japan. President Franklin D. Roosevelt hoped to persuade his fellow Americans that joining the war was the right thing to do.

OPPOSITE PAGE
The Japanese bombed an American fleet at Pearl Harbor, Hawaii, on December 7, 1941. On December 8, 1941, the United States officially entered World War II.
Courtesy of the National Archives and Records Administration.

The United States officially entered World War II on December 8, 1941, the day after Japanese bombers had destroyed the American fleet at Pearl Harbor, Hawaii. But in fact, Americans had been involved in military operations for most of 1941 and even earlier. By February 1941, the Battle of the Atlantic was raging between Germany and Great Britain. President Roosevelt moved the American "sea frontier" to the middle of the Atlantic, providing naval protection for British cargo ships. In June 1941, the German army advanced on Russia, quickly reaching the gates of Moscow. Fearing that the fall of Moscow would free Germany to launch new attacks on Great Britain, Roosevelt extended Lend-Lease (a program for supplying military equipment to the British) to include the Soviet Union. In July 1941, U.S. Marines landed on Iceland, preventing Germany from building a stronghold there. Throughout September and October 1941,

German submarines and destroyers attacked American ships. On October 30, 1941, the United States suffered its first major loss. German torpedoes sank the USS *Reuben James* in the Atlantic; over one hundred American lives were lost.

In East Asia, tensions had been rising since the early 1930s. Yet attempts were made to avoid war as late as 1941. In January of that year, a peace proposal offered the withdrawal of Japanese troops from China. But the U.S. government doubted the Japanese could stick to their promise. With war already destroying Europe, and tension rising around the world, American interventionists were gaining public approval. After the surprise Japanese attack on the American fleet at Pearl Harbor, the isolationist argument could no longer be taken seriously.

❖ ROOSEVELT RENAMED "DR. WIN-THE-WAR"

President Franklin D. Roosevelt had been pushing carefully for American involvement in World War II since fighting began in Europe in 1939. Between 1939 and 1941, huge resources had been directed to war-related manufacturing and the military. Roosevelt said that in the 1930s he had been "Dr. New Deal" (New Deal was the name given to his domestic policies during the 1930s). After Pearl Harbor, he became "Dr. Win-the-War." Because of the government resources already allocated for fighting a war, the United States was able to respond quickly.

Even so, the Pearl Harbor attack was a major setback for the U.S. Navy. For the first six months after December 1941, American forces struggled against the Japanese. On December 10, 1941, three days after Pearl Harbor, Japan destroyed the American air fleet at Clark Field in the Philippines. Japan then took the Philippines and quickly moved on to Thailand, Malaysia, and Singapore. American territories in the Pacific such as Guam and Wake Island were lost before Christmas. In February 1942, the American Pacific fleet was almost wiped out completely in the Battle of the Java Sea. The bombing of Tokyo, Japan, by a squadron of planes led by General James Doolittle (1896–1993) in April 1942 boosted morale, but few planes or U.S. soldiers survived the raid.

Although the attack on Tokyo was costly, it marked a turning point in the Pacific campaign. In May, American planes launched from the USS *Lexington* and USS *Yorktown* put three Japanese aircraft carriers out of action. Though the *Lexington* was lost, it was an important breakthrough. In June 1942, the Japanese fleet was stalled at the Battle of Midway; on August 7, American Marines landed on the island of Guadalcanal. Their fight with the Japanese for control of the Pacific would be long and brutal.

"Magic" was an electronic deciphering machine used by the U.S. government to crack the codes Japan used to send orders to its armed forces. Magic was so secret that the Special Intelligence Service (SIS) did not trust the White House to know about it. President Franklin D. Roosevelt was not allowed to read translated Japanese orders until January 23, 1941, 140 days after Magic was first used. On December 6, 1941, in Washington, D.C., at 1:00 P.M., Roosevelt sent a copy of a decoded Japanese message to U.S. Army Chief of Staff George C. Marshall. The message contained plans for a Japanese assault on American forces in the Pacific. Afraid that the Japanese might intercept normal military communications, Marshall sent a warning about the message to Pearl Harbor, Hawaii, by Western Union telegram. The message was not marked as urgent. The following morning, the Western Union office near Pearl Harbor sent a bicycle messenger to the naval base. He reached his destination at 11:45 A.M. local time, almost four hours after the Japanese attack had begun. The telegram finally reached the Pearl Harbor base commander at 4:00 P.M., long after the U.S. fleet had been destroyed.

Neither side was willing to take prisoners. Marines burned surrendering Japanese with flame-throwers and put severed heads of enemy soldiers on stakes. Casualties were horrific on both sides. In the spring of 1945 alone, 130,000 Japanese and nearly 15,000 Americans lost their lives at Iwo Jima and Okinawa.

But although the fight with Japan would last another two years, by 1943 the balance had shifted in favor of the United States. After the disastrous Battle of Leyte Gulf, the Japanese were desperate. They trained teenage boys to fly planes but not to land them; instead, they crashed their planes into American ships. These strategies, called kamikaze missions, were seen by Americans as a sign of Japanese fanaticism and savagery.

Roosevelt's policy of building up the military and armaments manufacturing made America's intervention in the war much more successful than it might have been. But although the American public was strongly behind the fight against Japan, the Roosevelt administration had to be more careful in entering North Africa and Europe. In Egypt, British troops

*American general
George S. Patton helped
lead the United States
and the Allied forces to
victory in World War II.*
*Courtesy of the Library
of Congress.*

had been struggling against German tank divisions since early 1941. Then in October 1942, led by General Bernard Montgomery (1887–1976), the British defeated the Germans at El Alamein. Over fourteen thousand British lives were lost in just four days, but German losses were heavier.

In November, with German General Erwin Rommel (1891–1944) in slow retreat, American Marines led Operation Torch, a troop landing on the Moroccan and Algerian coasts. Its planner, Dwight D. Eisenhower (1890–1969), would later become Supreme Allied Commander in Europe because of this operation's success. The battle for the empty deserts of North Africa seemed pointless to some. But it made possible the later invasion of Italy, forcing the resignation of Italian fascist leader Benito Mussolini (1883–1945). Operation Torch is often seen by military historians as a practice run for the invasion of France by American and British troops in 1944. Lessons learned on the North African beaches undoubtedly saved many lives in later campaigns.

❖ ALLIED LEADERS PLAN EUROPEAN INVASION STRATEGY

After January 1942, President Franklin D. Roosevelt met regularly with British Prime Minister Winston Churchill (1874–1965) to plan strategy. Soviet leader Joseph Stalin (1879–1953) was the third Allied leader, but he had difficulty traveling to summit meetings. The partnership with the Soviets was in any case never likely to last beyond the end of the war. Some American and British strategists had even considered siding with Nazi Germany against Russia prior to 1939.

In Stalin's absence, Roosevelt and Churchill worked on plans for the invasion of northern France at the Quebec conference in August 1943. Stalin agreed to the plans, hoping that such an invasion would draw German troops away from the bloody Russian front. But it was not possible for Britain to conduct the invasion alone. The high risk of heavy American casualties made it difficult for Roosevelt to justify an immediate invasion for political reasons, however. When Roosevelt and Churchill finally met with Stalin in Tehran, Iran, late in 1943, they told Stalin that his Russian troops would have to continue fighting the German army for some time to come.

Roosevelt gambled on the Russians being able to weaken the German army so that fewer American troops would die in the invasion of Europe. The gamble paid off. On June 6, 1944, now known as D-Day, Operation Overlord moved 150,000 American and British troops onto the beaches of northern France. The troops faced later setbacks, such as the Battle of the Bulge in the forests of Belgium. But with German forces weakened in the onslaught, the Allies' armies moved steadily across northern Europe toward Germany. As the troops advanced, British and American bombers flattened factories, oil depots, and cities in the German heartland. In February 1945, the city of Dresden was firebombed, killing 135,000 civilians. This was almost three times the number of people killed by the atomic bomb dropped on Hiroshima, Japan a few months later.

The Yalta Conference

Between February 4 and 11, 1945, Franklin D. Roosevelt, Winston Churchill, and Joseph Stalin met at Yalta (a port city on the Black Sea in the republic of Ukraine in the Soviet Union). The three Allied leaders needed to decide what to do when the war ended. They discussed future European borders and the postwar governments of Poland, Germany, and other countries in Eastern Europe. At the time of the conference, the Soviet Red Army was moving quickly toward Berlin, Germany. Roosevelt knew that, having lost millions of men, the Soviets would not want to hand back territory they had gained during the fighting. More than anything, Roosevelt wanted to insure free democratic government and free markets throughout Europe and East Asia. He gave land to Stalin in return for reassurances about Soviet future plans. But when Roosevelt died on April 12, 1945, his successors were not so generous. The postwar world as envisaged at Yalta was seen by later U.S. politicians as a sellout of American interests.

The ruthless burning of Dresden has since been interpreted as revenge for the destruction of Coventry, Hull, and other British cities. But the effect of the Allied bombing on German morale was profound. Berlin, the German capital, lay in ruins; on April 30, 1945, Nazi leader Adolf Hitler shot himself dead. On May 7, the German army surrendered. Although Roosevelt had died a month earlier, on April 12, his careful management of the war effort in part had achieved this total and unconditional surrender.

❖ ATOMIC BOMBS END THE WAR IN THE PACIFIC

In the spring of 1945, fighting in the Pacific was at its fiercest. It was feared that a push to invade Japan itself would cost more than one million American lives. American government strategists knew they had to avoid such shocking losses. American bombers had been pounding targets on the Japanese mainland for many months with some success. But on July 16, 1945 a new weapon became available. On that day, the first atomic bomb was exploded at Alamogordo, New Mexico. On August 6, an atomic bomb, code-named "Little Boy," was dropped on the Japanese city of Hiroshima, killing fifty thousand people in a few seconds.

The Japanese were confused. All communication with Hiroshima was lost instantly. Not realizing the power of this new weapon, the Japanese allowed the August 8 deadline for surrender issued by the United States to pass. On August 9, a second Japanese city, Nagasaki, was flattened by a second atomic bomb, code-named "Fat Man." Unconditional surrender followed on August 15, 1945, known ever since as Victory in Japan (V-J) Day. The most destructive and lethal war in human history was over.

Although the atomic bombs ended the war, President Harry S Truman had problems justifying his decision to use nuclear weapons. Important military figures, such as the army's general Dwight D. Eisenhower and the navy's admiral of the fleet William D. Leahy (1875–1959), opposed the idea. Truman argued that by shortening the conflict, the bombs saved more lives than they destroyed. But in fact, Japan was on the brink of collapse anyway. Its navy had been completely destroyed, many of its factories had stopped operating, and its army was cut off. So, while Truman's argument was partly true, other political reasons also came into play.

On August 6, 1945, the United States dropped an atomic bomb on the city of Hiroshima, Japan. Fifty thousand people were killed and World War II ended less than ten days later when Japan surrendered. **Reproduced by permission of Getty Images.**

The first was that the Manhattan Project, which developed the atomic bomb, had cost $2 billion. Some officials, including General George C. Marshall, thought failure to use the bomb would be a waste of money and would damage the administration. Secondly, and more importantly, Truman wanted to prevent the Soviets from taking over Japan. The whole plan to rebuild and exploit a free market in East Asia depended on a swift end to hostilities. If the Red Army had taken Japan, a new conflict within a few years seemed certain. With the American public unwilling to see many thousands more young men slaughtered, the atomic bomb appeared to be the only solution. In the end, some of the warnings from Truman's critics came true. Dropping the atomic bombs on Japan began an international era of fear and distrust, and the threat of global annihilation.

❖ CIVIL LIBERTIES CHALLENGED BY WAR

Civil liberties, or fundamental individual rights protected by law, and personal freedoms are usually the first casualties of war. During the Civil War (1861–65), President Abraham Lincoln (1809–1865) allowed defendants to be imprisoned without being charged with a specific crime. In World War I, President Woodrow Wilson (1856–1924) restricted political activity and free speech. World War II was no exception. But although it removed some freedoms, the Roosevelt administration also convinced many Americans that giving up their civil liberties was a matter of national pride.

Even before the United States officially entered the war, the federal government began to put pressure on civil liberties. Enacted by Congress and signed by President Franklin D. Roosevelt in 1940, the Alien Registration Act (also known as the Smith Act) made it illegal to hold certain political opinions or to talk about them publicly. The first convictions under the act took place in 1944. Eighteen hard-line communists, known as Trotskyites, from Minnesota were sentenced to between twelve and eighteen months in jail. Their crime was they had spoken out against the war aims of the U.S. government. Curiously, the Communist Party of the U.S.A. (CPUSA) supported the trial and the conviction.

Although the Smith Act was repealed in 1948, it was reenacted later the same year. President Harry S Truman, desperate to show he was not soft on communists, directed the Justice Department to bring the eleven members of the National Board of the CPUSA to trial. They were convicted of making anti-American statements in 1949 and released on bail. Two appellate court decisions upheld the Smith Act's restrictions and, in 1951, four of the eleven convicts jumped bail.

After the Japanese attack on Pearl Harbor on December 7, 1941, Japanese Americans discovered that their civil liberties and rights as U.S. citizens were not guaranteed. On March 31, 1942, Japanese Americans on the West Coast were ordered to report to control stations. From there they were taken to camps where they were interned (held captive). Between 1942 and 1945, ten camps held around 120,000 people from the western states. They were allowed to bring with them only what they could carry, and they were forced to sell their houses, land, and automobiles at very low prices. In 1983, a report calculated that Japanese American citizens lost $6.2 billion in property and earnings (at 1983 prices) during the three-year period. It was not until 1988 that the U.S. Congress issued a formal apology for the internment to Japanese Americans.

Throughout the 1940s, American courts struggled with the problems of free speech and internment. African Americans actually saw some improvement in their civil rights during the decade. The 1944 *Smith* v. *Allwright* ruling banned an all-white Democratic primary in Texas, while black leader Adam Clayton Powell (1908–1972) was elected to the U.S. Congress in the same year. Meanwhile, the Supreme Court took steps to limit the power of the authorities over individual citizens. Overall, however, civil liberties were eroded in the United States during the 1940s. The Smith Act and the internment of Japanese Americans were both wartime measures. But after 1945 further legal challenges would come from efforts to control the spread of communism.

❖ WAR AGAINST FASCISM ENDS IN WAR AGAINST COMMUNISM

Throughout World War II, the Soviet Union was a useful ally of the United States and Great Britain. Though the Soviets had been enemies of the West since they seized power in Russia in 1917, for the duration of the war, the Allies united against fascism (government by dictators). But as the war drew to a close, it became clear that the postwar goals of the Allies were different. Britain wanted to hang onto its empire, while the United States wanted to make sure international free trade survived. The Soviet Union's aim was to expand its borders.

Until 1945, the Soviet leader Joseph Stalin (1879–1953) went along with plans agreed to between President Roosevelt and British Prime Minister Winston Churchill. But at Potsdam, Germany in July 1945, everything changed. Roosevelt, who had died on April 12 of that year, had been replaced by President Harry S Truman, while Churchill had lost the British general election to Clement Attlee (1883–1967). Truman was less friendly toward Stalin than Roosevelt had been, and Stalin himself came

The Arms Race Begins

When the United States exploded the first atomic bomb in a test in the New Mexico desert on July 16, 1945, American politicians knew they now had a great advantage over the Soviet Union. When the Potsdam conference began the following day, President Harry S Truman could begin negotiations knowing he had the answer to the battle-hardened Soviet Red Army, poised to move in on Japanese territory. But it was impossible to keep the technology secret for long. Despite attempts to control atomic weapons production, the Soviet Union developed its own atomic bomb in 1949. Spies were believed to have stolen the technology from American research facilities. The atmosphere of secrecy and distrust grew more intense on both sides. Within a matter of months, a nuclear arms race was underway.

to the conference with a tougher agenda. Both Truman and Attlee were convinced Stalin was planning world conquest. Stalin believed the same of them.

After Potsdam, an uneasy truce existed as Europe and Asia were divided up between the three Allied powers. The atomic bomb, which was used to end the war with Japan, added a further element of tension. In 1946, Britain's ex-prime minister Churchill made a speech at Westminster College in Fulton, Missouri, declaring that "an iron curtain has descended" across Europe. A year later, George F. Kennan (1904–), an American diplomat stationed in Moscow, Russia, wrote a paper explaining that the Soviet Union had to expand its borders to survive. Kennan urged President Truman to take steps to contain Soviet expansion, and a cold-war term came into common use: containment.

By 1948, the lines of the cold war had been drawn. The United States, Britain, and France controlled West Germany, and the Soviet Union controlled East Germany. The city of Berlin, now completely surrounded by Soviet territory, was also divided into four zones. On June 24, 1948, the Soviets blockaded overland routes into West Berlin, forcing the other three Allies to fly in food and supplies. As tensions rose, one hundred B-29 bombers, ready to drop atomic bombs onto the Soviet Union, were deployed in Britain. Stalin backed down and reopened the overland routes, but this incident was the beginning of forty years of cold war.

Gradually, the cold war became a part of the political landscape. The North Atlantic Treaty Organization (NATO) was established on April 4, 1949. NATO's twelve member countries formed an organized military alliance against the Soviet Union. The military tension, and fears of Soviet expansion, made anticommunist feeling a major influence on postwar politics in the United States.

❖ CONGRESS SEEKS OUT SUBVERSIVES

The House Un-American Activities Committee (HUAC) first began conducting its investigations in 1930 as the Fish Committee. Its job was to uncover anti-American activities among U.S. citizens. In January 1945, the special Fish committee became a standing committee of the House and got its new name. In Public Law 601, Congress gave HUAC permission to investigate activities that might threaten the nation's security. The vague language used to define such activities in the bill meant that the law was open to abuse.

The film industry was HUAC's first high-profile target. From the mid-1930s onwards, many Hollywood actors, directors, writers, and other per-

The House Un-American Activities Committee targeted Hollywood for potential Communists because of their influence in the media. The "Hollywood Ten" were ten Hollywood actors, screenwriters, producers, and directors blacklisted by HUAC. Reproduced by permission of AP/Wide World Photos.

sonnel joined the Communist Party of the U.S.A. (CPUSA). During World War II, while the Soviet Union and the United States were allies, this was not really an issue. But when the policy of containment (preventing Soviet territorial expansion) came into force in 1947, the U.S. government became very wary of card-carrying Communists in positions of influence. Some HUAC members, such as J. Parnell Thomas (1895–1970), also worried that communist propaganda was appearing in Hollywood movies.

Between October 28 and 30, 1947, HUAC interviewed many actors, writers, and directors as part of an investigation into their political leanings. A total of forty-one people were interviewed, and nineteen were classified as "unfriendly" to the government. Every witness was eventually asked the question: "Are you now, or have you ever been, a member of the Communist Party of the United States of America?" Ten witnesses refused to answer the questions and were found guilty of contempt of court by a grand jury in April 1948. Ironically, they were sent to the same prison as ex-HUAC chairman Thomas, who had been convicted of corruption.

HUAC activities in the 1940s marked the beginning of over a decade of anticommunist witch hunting. American politics in the late 1940s and early 1950s was dominated by the fear of communists and the search for spies and subversives. HUAC did not have the powers of the Senate Permanent Investigations Subcommittee under Joseph McCarthy (1908–1957). But together, these two investigations kept questions of individual rights, free speech, and national security at the forefront of American politics and law in the late 1940s and 1950s.

For More Information

BOOKS

Ambrose, Stephen E. *Citizen Soldiers: The U.S. Army from the Normandy Beaches to the Bulge to the Surrender of Germany, June 7, 1944–May 7, 1945.* New York: Simon & Schuster, 1998.

Anderson, Dale. *The Cold War Years.* Austin, TX: Raintree Steck-Vaughn Publishers, 2001.

Cayton, Andrew, Elizabeth I. Perry, and Allan M. Winkler. *America: Pathways to the Present: America in the Twentieth Century.* New York: Prentice Hall School Group, 1998.

Chronicle of the Twentieth Century. Mount Cisco, NY: Chronicle, 1994.

Collier, Christopher. *Progressivism, the Great Depression, and the New Deal, 1901 to 1941.* New York: Benchmark Books/Marshall Cavendish, 2000.

Collier, Christopher, and James Lincoln Collier. *The United States in the Cold War.* New York: Benchmark Books/Marshall Cavendish, 2001.

Cook, Chris, and David Waller, eds. *The Longman Handbook of Modern American History, 1763–1996.* New York: Longman, 1998.

Cozic, Charles P., ed. *Civil Liberties: Opposing Viewpoints.* San Diego, CA: Greenhaven Press, 1994.

Decade of Triumph: The 40s. Alexandria, VA: Time-Life Books, 1999.

Donovan, Robert J. *The Second Victory: The Marshall Plan and the Postwar Revival of Europe.* New York: Madison Books, 1987.

Dorman, Michael. *Witch Hunt: The Underside of American Democracy.* New York: Delacorte Press, 1976.

Fariello, Griffin. *Red Scare: Memories of the American Inquisition, An Oral History.* New York: Norton, 1995.

Feinstein, Stephen. *The 1940s From World War II to Jackie Robinson.* Berkeley Heights, NJ: Enslow Publishers, 2000.

Grant, R.G. *Hiroshima and Nagasaki.* Austin, TX: Raintree Steck-Vaughn, 1998.

Hall, Kermit L. *The Oxford Companion to the Supreme Court.* New York: Oxford University Press, 1992.

Hills, Ken. *1940s.* Austin, TX: Raintree Steck-Vaughn, 1992.

Isaacs, Sally Senzell. *America in the Time of Franklin Delano Roosevelt: The Story of Our Nation from Coast to Coast, from 1929 to 1948.* Des Plaines, IL: Heinemann Library, 2000.

Isaacs, Sally Senzell. *The Rise to World Power, 1929 to 1948.* Des Plaines IL: Heinemann Library, 1999.

Larsen, Rebecca. *Franklin D. Roosevelt: Man of Destiny.* New York: Franklin Watts, 1991.

McCauley, Martin. *The Origins of the Cold War 1941–1949.* New York: Addison Wesley, 1996.

O'Neal, Michael. *President Truman and the Atomic Bomb: Opposing Viewpoints.* San Diego, CA: Greenhaven Press, 1990.

Schuman, Michael A. *Harry S Truman.* New York: Enslow, 1997.

Selden, Kyoko, and Mark Selden, eds. *The Atomic Bomb: Voices From Hiroshima and Nagasaki.* Armonk, NY: M.E. Sharpe, 1989.

Sherrow, Victoria. *Hiroshima.* New York: New Discovery Books, 1994.

Sifakis, Carl. *The Encyclopedia of American Crime.* New York: Facts on File, 1982.

Terkel, Studs. *"The Good War": An Oral History of World War Two.* New York: Pantheon Books, 1984.

Wood, Tim, and R.J. Unstead. *The 1940s.* New York: Franklin Watts, 1990.

WEB SITES

FDR Library and Digital Archives: K12 Learning Center. [Online] http://www.fdrlibrary.marist.edu/teach.html (accessed March, 2002).

Truman Presidential Museum and Library. [Online] http://www.trumanlibrary.org/index.html (accessed March, 2002).

chapter five **Lifestyles and Social Trends**

1940: A new kind of glass improves visibility through automobile windshields by 62 percent.

1940: Architect Frank Lloyd Wright completes the People's Church in Kansas City.

1940: Americans own 69 percent of the world's cars.

1940: Colorfast textiles are introduced, making clothes more durable during washing.

1941: May 22 Pope Pius XII warns that wearing "daring" dresses can be dangerous for the souls of Catholic girls.

1941: June 25 President Roosevelt signs Executive Order 8802, banning racial discrimination in the defense industries and setting up the Fair Employment Practices Committee.

1942: April 14 The *Saturday Evening Post* denies that an article called "The Case Against the Jew" is anti-Semitic (prejudiced against Jews).

1943: Sales of Bibles are up 25 percent.

1943: Long-distance telephone calls are restricted to a maximum of five minutes.

1943: Companies introduce piped-in music, coffee breaks, and suggestion boxes to make up for long working hours in wartime factories.

1943: Teenagers enjoy slumber parties, beach parties, and dates at soda shops and hamburger "joints."

1943: June 20 Race riots break out in Detroit and last for forty-eight hours.

1943: April 26 U.S. Jews begin a six-week period of prayer and mourning for European Jews killed by the Nazis.

1944: Air-conditioning is introduced in American automobiles.

1944: Fifty-eight percent of women between the ages of twenty and twenty-four are married.

1944: January 2 The Federal Council of Churches announces that 68,501,186 Americans are members of 256 religious groups.

1944: May 18 The number of Catholics in the United States increases by 46,222 over the previous year. The total stands at 23,419,701.

1945: Eighty percent of the eighteen million women who work outside the home say they want to continue working after the war ends.

1945: Many schools have air-raid drills.

1945: April 12 President Roosevelt dies at Warm Springs, Georgia. Vice President

Harry S Truman becomes the thirty-third president of the United States.

1945: **August 6** A hydrogen bomb, with a picture of movie actress Rita Hayworth wearing a bathing suit, is dropped on the Bikini Islands in the Pacific. Four days later, Hayworth's bathing suit is named after the islands.

1946: *Life* magazine reports that consumers have begun a frenzy of shopping.

1946: The Franklin D. Roosevelt dime goes into circulation.

1946: With the birth rate 20 percent higher than 1945, the baby boom begins. Seventy-four percent of couples have their first child within their first year of marriage.

1946: RCA puts a television set with a ten-inch screen on sale to the public. It costs $374.

1946: **July 2** Blacks vote in the Mississippi Democratic primary for the first time since Reconstruction.

1947: Vogue magazine compares the new Oldsmobile design with the modern architecture of Frank Lloyd Wright.

1947: The Dead Sea Scrolls are discovered by two Bedouin boys in a cave in British-occupied Palestine.

1947: **January** The number of war veterans in college peaks at 1.2 million. The college population reaches an all-time high of 6.1 million students.

1947: **June 11** Ice-cream sales rocket when sugar rationing ends.

1948: **January 10** A Gallup poll reveals that 94 percent of Americans believe in God.

1948: **August 1** A record 77,386,188 Americans are church members. This shows a gain of more than 3 million in just two years.

1948: **September 28** The construction firm Levitt and Sons sells fifty-three houses on Long Island at a total cost of $1.1 million, a new world record for house-selling on one day. By the end of the week, the company has sold an additional forty-seven houses.

1949: For the first time since 1927, Chrysler is able to announce sales of more than $1 million.

1949: **January** For the first time, black people attend events surrounding a presidential inauguration in Washington, D.C., African Americans even stay in the same hotels as whites.

1949: **September 25** Religious leader Billy Graham begins an evangelical revival in Los Angeles. More than 350,000 people attend his meetings.

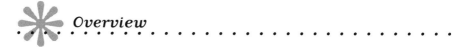

Overview

The United States did not enter World War II (1939–45) until after the Japanese attack on Pearl Harbor on December 7, 1941. But even before that, the war had made an impact on American life. Manufacturers began to put more effort into supplying the wartime needs of Europe, creating shortages at home. By 1941, raw materials such as steel, rubber, nylon, silk, oil, and fabrics were in short supply. Automobile manufacturers gradually converted their factories to build airplanes, tanks, and other military vehicles. Clothing manufacturers made uniforms for the military. Shortages also changed the way civilian goods were designed. In order to use less fabric, clothes became tighter and more versatile. Buildings were simpler and more efficient, while furniture became less elaborate and more functional.

After 1941, American life began to change in many important ways. Rural dwellers moved to the cities to work in factories. They included millions of women, ethnic minorities, and teenagers. These groups had never worked together before, so there was often tension between them. Wartime jobs paid well, so many Americans found themselves better off than ever before. Yet wartime shortages meant that Americans at home had very little on which to spend their money. Instead, they bought war bonds or saved in other ways. After the war, these savings fueled a period of consumerism more intense than any other in history.

Postwar consumerism was even stronger because of the shortages that had occurred earlier. In fashion, the war years forced designers to find ways of using every inch of cloth. The U.S. government put limits on the amount of fabric available for civilian clothes. Women's clothing was tailored and elegant, but dresses and suits in wartime were kept simple. Pockets, frills, and unnecessary buttons disappeared. To make up for a lack of adornments, women wore hats and high heels, and carried long, flat leather handbags. Shortages affected men's fashion even more dramatically. Suits were simple, two-piece garments, with squared-off shoulders. But because most producers of clothes for men were making military uniforms, it was almost impossible to buy a new suit after 1942. After the war ended, clothes became more luxurious. Men wore gray and brown suits with white shirts and slim ties. Fabrics were heavy and expensive. After work, American men relaxed in comfortable slacks, sweaters, and sportswear. For American women, a style called the New Look brought full skirts and soft, feminine curves to fashion.

After the war, manufacturers applied new skills and ideas to making goods for the civilian market. Cars were large, powerful, and streamlined. New materials, such as nylon, went into making carpets, furniture, and even ornaments. Everywhere, designs reflected the confidence of a wealthy nation building its new identity as a world leader. Glittering skyscrapers expressed the confident mood of corporate America, while sprawling new suburbs offered home ownership to the expanding middle class.

More than anything else, Americans wanted to put the war behind them and enjoy the benefits of victory. Many women stayed in the workforce when the war ended, but the emphasis was on home, family, and traditional values. The United States was the only nation that had fought in the war to see church attendance increase sharply when the fighting ended. Though prosperity brought new moral challenges, all the major U.S. religious groups gained strength in the 1940s. There was a huge increase in financial contributions, and church building expanded rapidly. The affluence of the 1950s resulted in large part from technological advances made during the war. But it was also a result of Americans' desire to rebuild a stable, more secure society for themselves and their children.

Hannah Arendt (1906–1975) Best known for her book *The Origins of Totalitarianism* (1951), Hannah Arendt also published many articles on politics and philosophy. Imprisoned by the Nazis in 1933, she lived in Paris before escaping to New York in 1941. She spent the 1940s and 1950s studying totalitarianism, and concluded that the Nazis were not evil or psychopathic, but just thoughtless and crude. Her frightening message was that every human being is capable of the cruelty and violence that was carried out by the Nazis. *Photo reproduced by permission of AP/Wide World Photos.*

Marcel Breuer (1902–1981) Marcel Breuer moved to the United States from Germany in 1937. His style as an architect was to combine wood and brick with more contemporary materials such as metal and concrete. He designed many houses and residential blocks in America throughout the 1940s. Among his most notable designs are the Aluminum City Terrace Housing buildings (1942) in New Kensington, Pennsylvania, and the Robinson House (1947) in Williamstown, Massachusetts. In 1968, Breuer was awarded the American Institute of Architects' Gold Medal, its highest award. *Photo courtesy of the Library of Congress.*

Mary McLeod Bethune (1875–1955) For more than three decades, Mary McLeod Bethune was the most influential black woman in America. She believed that African Americans should organize themselves through the government to fight racism. In 1904, she established the Daytona Normal and Industrial Institute, which became Bethune-Cookman College after World War I (1914–18). In 1943, the college bestowed its first four-year degrees on graduates in teacher education. Bethune was also a renowned civil rights leader, working closely with the federal government to get black workers into the defense industries in the 1940s. She was an active civil rights campaigner until her death. *Photo reproduced by permission of the Corbis Corporation.*

James Farmer (1920–1999) In 1942, James Farmer cofounded the Congress of Racial Equality (CORE) and was its national director until 1966. Through CORE, he brought nonviolent protest tactics to the civil rights movement, and in doing so inspired some of its most impressive victories. CORE's first successful sit-in was at a restaurant in Chicago in 1943. Multiracial protesters occupied seats reserved for members of specific races. During the 1960s, Farmer became involved with encouraging eligible black people to register to vote. He left CORE in 1966 when younger members began arguing for a separate black state. *Photo reproduced by permission of Fisk University Library.*

Claire McCardell (1905–1958) Claire McCardell's first clothing collection, released in 1941, introduced American fashion to the idea that sportswear could be designed for any occasion. She put as much care into designing, and used similar materials for everything from bathing suits to evening dresses. She was particularly well known for her "Popover" housedress, designed to withstand the wear and tear of housework. During the war, she introduced ballet slippers as accessories to get around restrictions on the use of shoe leather. She won many awards, including the Women's National Press Club Award (1950). *Photo reproduced by permission of the Corbis Corporation.*

Robert Moses (1888–1981) For nearly forty years Robert Moses helped shape the landscape of New York City. His projects were sometimes beneficial, but just as frequently damaging to urban life. In 1920, he submitted a plan for the improvement of parks and highways in the city. Many of the parks and public spaces he commissioned in the 1930s were accessible only by car, earning him a reputation for helping only the wealthy. Moses' plans for new highways eased travel into the city, but they also destroyed established neighborhoods. More positively, as New York City parks commissioner from 1934 to 1960, Moses built over six hundred new playgrounds and city parks. *Photo reproduced by permission of Getty Images.*

Reinhold Niebuhr (1892–1971) Like his German-born father, Reinhold Niebuhr studied at the Eden Theological Seminary in Wellston, Missouri. In 1913, he took over his father's pulpit in Lincoln, Illinois. But within a few years he had stepped out from his father's shadow. Niebuhr became well known as a theologian of the liberal left, arguing that Christian theology was a better framework for understanding society than Marxism or other political philosophies. In later life, he became a figurehead of the establishment. But in 1969, his ideas were still radical enough for him to be investigated by the Federal Bureau of Investigation (FBI). *Photo courtesy of the Library of Congress.*

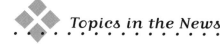

Topics in the News . . . .

❖ AMERICANS EMBRACE THE INTERNATIONAL STYLE IN ARCHITECTURE

So-called modern architecture was popular in Europe during the 1930s, but it did not arrive in the United States until World War II (1939–45). The modern style favored clean, functional lines, and used construction materials such as steel and glass to create flat, machine-like surfaces. Because it was used around the world, this kind of architecture became known as the International Style.

One reason International Style architecture arrived in the United States in the late 1930s and early 1940s was immigration. Many modernist architects fled to the United States in the 1930s after Adolf Hitler (1889–1945) came to power in Germany. Walter Gropius (1883–1969) became dean of the architecture school at Harvard University, and hired his colleague from Germany, Marcel Breuer (1902–1981). Another colleague of Gropius, László Moholy-Nagy (1895–1946), taught at the Institute of Design in Chicago, while Eero Saarinen (1910–1961) taught at Cranbrook Academy of Art in Bloomfield Hills, Michigan.

The International Style adapted itself to the American setting and changed in the process. Alvar Aalto (1898–1976), who worked at the Massachusetts Institute of Technology, built a red-brick dormitory building known as the Baker House (1948), which curved along the Charles River. More radical than this was the Glass House (1949), designed by American-born Philip Johnson (1906–); the building's walls were made entirely of glass. Despite its rigid, squared-off lines, the Glass House blended in well with the surrounding landscape of New Canaan, Connecticut.

But the architect who did the most to define the style of the 1940s was Ludwig Mies van der Rohe (1886–1969). He arrived in the United States in 1937, and pioneered techniques of building a thin "skin" of glass over a steel or concrete "skeleton" of the building's structure. His first stand-alone buildings in the United States were the Promontory Apartments (1948–49), and apartment towers at 860-880 Lake Shore Drive in Chicago. Both of these buildings used ribbons of glass over a steel frame. This version of the International Style, known as Miesian architecture, became a symbol of corporate power. In Portland, Oregon, the Equitable Savings and Loan building (1948) used a skin of polished aluminum over a reinforced concrete frame, while Saarinen's General Motors Technical Center in Warren, Michigan (1948–65), drew on the design of Mies van der Rohe's buildings on the campus of the Illinois Institute of Technology (1939–41).

Besides the arrival of European architects, World War II had produced other effects on American architecture. During the Great Depression many architects struggled to find work, and the situation did not improve in the early 1940s. In April 1942, the War Production Board (WPB) issued Order L-41, ending all construction other than that of buildings essential to the war effort. The Supply Priorities and Allocations Board (SPAB) put strict limits on the materials that could be used. The "skin-over-skeleton" techniques favored by International Style architects proved useful for low-cost housing projects and for military bases. Channel Heights in San Diego, California (1943), by Richard Neutra (1892–1970), and Aluminum City Terrace in New Kensington, Pennsylvania (1941), by Gropius and Breuer, are among the most distinguished examples of this spartan modern style.

Architects also were employed in wartime, designing factories, temporary housing for refugees in Europe and for military troops abroad, and detention camps. They designed housing delivered in ready-made parts that could be bolted together on site. One such building was based on a circular sheet-steel grain bin. Known popularly as "Igloos," these houses were easily transported and very strong. It was predicted that when the war ended, four hundred thousand new houses would be needed immediately, with demand rising to one million a year by the late 1940s. Some commentators expected "Igloos" to become a common sight in American cities. After difficult times in the 1930s and early 1940s, American architects in the second half of the decade found themselves in great demand.

❖ FASHION GOES TO WAR

World War II had a dramatic effect on American fashion. Restrictions on materials such as silk, nylon, rubber, and leather changed the way clothes were made and the way they were worn. Government Order L-85, announced in 1943, stated that a maximum of one-and-three-fourth yards of fabric could be used in a dress. The only clothing styles unaffected by L-85 were wedding dresses, religious vestments, infant wear, and maternity wear. As supplies of fabric, buttons, and fasteners disappeared, American fashion was forced to change.

For men, shortages of fabrics meant that civilian suits became simpler. Gone was the double-breasted, three-piece suit of the 1930s. Instead, men in the 1940s wore the two-piece suit, with narrower lapels on the jacket and no cuffs or pleats in the pants. But in 1941, men's clothing manufacturers limited their production to military uniforms almost exclusively. Before long it was difficult to find a suit of any kind in stores. Even after the war ended, clothes for men remained scarce because of the overwhelming demand caused by millions of soldiers returning to civilian society.

The effect of Order L-85 on women's clothes was also dramatic. Fabric shortages led to narrower waistlines, shorter skirts, and blouses without

The League of Broke Husbands

The New Look was highly popular after the drab fashions of the war years. But not all women thought it was a good thing. Twenty-four-year-old Bobbie Woodward of Dallas did not want to hide her legs as the new fashions required. And she did not see why her husband should have to buy her a complete new wardrobe. In August 1947, she founded the Little Below-the-Knee (LBK) club. LBK branches sprang up across the country. Its members picketed America's downtown stores, chanting "The Alamo fell, but our hemlines will not!" The high prices of New Look fashions annoyed men, too. One group formed the League of Broke Husbands to protest the way the fashion industry was manipulating them into spending their hard-earned money.

cuffs or pockets. Scarves and hoods were expensive and difficult to justify. For both women and men, blends such as rayon gabardine became the most common wool substitute. Women suffered most from restrictions on silk and nylon, the materials used to make stockings. Japan slashed its exports of silk in the late 1930s, and when war broke out supplies stopped altogether. Nylon, the alternative material to silk, first appeared in 1939. But within a few months of the first retail sales of nylon stockings, wholesale supplies of nylon were commandeered by the government.

Most of the garment industry's effort during wartime went into making military uniforms. Uniforms had to be durable, quick-drying, and adaptable. In the tropics, soldiers wore loose cotton shirts, while nylon netting helped protect them from insects. In Europe, American troops wore a uniform consisting of an olive-colored wool service shirt and trousers with a water-repellent M43 field jacket. Boots were high-laced, with a buckle ankle flap to protect the trouser bottoms in wet conditions. Foot soldiers could wear out a pair of boots in a month, causing a shortage of leather at home. There were tight restrictions on the amount of leather that could be used in civilian shoes.

Women served in the military as nurses, clerical workers, pilots, and coast-guard recruits. Images of women in uniform filled the media. Six million women also went to work in war industries, such as ship and aircraft manufacturing. Most women in these jobs wore the same clothes as

OPPOSITE PAGE
Although women in the service, like members of the Women's Army Corps, wore their uniforms with pride during the work day, they wore more feminine clothing after work. **Courtesy of the National Archives and Records Administration.**

their male counterparts. But at Boeing, fashion designer Muriel King (1900–1977) designed special overalls for women. Boeing liked the overalls because they used a minimum of fabric and were therefore cheap. Workers liked the "slimming waistlines" and flattering cut. After work, women went back to wearing more feminine clothes, including belted dresses in printed fabrics.

During the war, designers made sticking to supply limits a matter of national pride. But after 1945, clothes became more luxurious. In spring 1947, French designer Christian Dior (1905–1957) introduced his "New Look," a style that has come to define the fashion of the late 1940s and the 1950s. Skirts were longer and fuller, with a "wasp" waistline. Soft, full collars and sleeves, sloping shoulder lines, and padded bras emphasized the feminine shape. While other designers such as Hollywood's Gilbert Adrian (1903–1959) created practical but feminine clothes, Dior's designs pushed women back into their traditional roles. For men, too, the postwar years brought a return to tradition. Emphasizing men's return to the workplace, the gray flannel suit was the dominant male fashion of the late 1940s. With its three-button jacket, small lapels, and flat-front pants, the gray flannel suit also marked the rise of corporate America in the postwar world.

❖ WAR TRANSFORMS THE FAMILY

Around six million women joined the American labor force during the war. They took the place of men who had been drafted into the military. In the mid-1930s, 80 percent of Americans disapproved of women working outside the home. By 1942, only 42 percent saw it as a negative development. Sixty-nine percent of married working women wanted to keep their jobs after the war despite the fact that they were paid less than men. After the Japanese attack on Pearl Harbor thousands of couples applied for marriage licenses. In 1942, the government even encouraged couples to marry by providing a "family allotment" of extra pay for families of men in the military. Separation brought obvious problems for couples and their young families, spurring a desire for security and comfort in the postwar years. The government's position was that, in peacetime, a woman's place was in the home. Sociologist Willard Waller (1899–1945) argued that mothers who worked were creating a generation of juvenile delinquents. He suggested that the independent woman was "out of hand."

Children, as well as adults, were affected by the war. For one thing, there were many more of them in America than ever before. Couples often conceived a "goodbye baby" before the man went off to fight, so that by 1943 the U.S. birthrate was at a sixteen-year peak. It was the

*OPPOSITE PAGE
Images like "Rosie the
Riveter" were supposed
to encourage women to
be strong while their
husbands and male
relatives were in combat.
Reproduced by permission of
Random House, Inc.*

beginning of a "baby boom," which lasted until the early 1960s. In the long run, children usually adapted well to having absent fathers, but they often suffered anxiety and uncertainty in the short term. Sixteen million men were separated from their families by the war, and many children

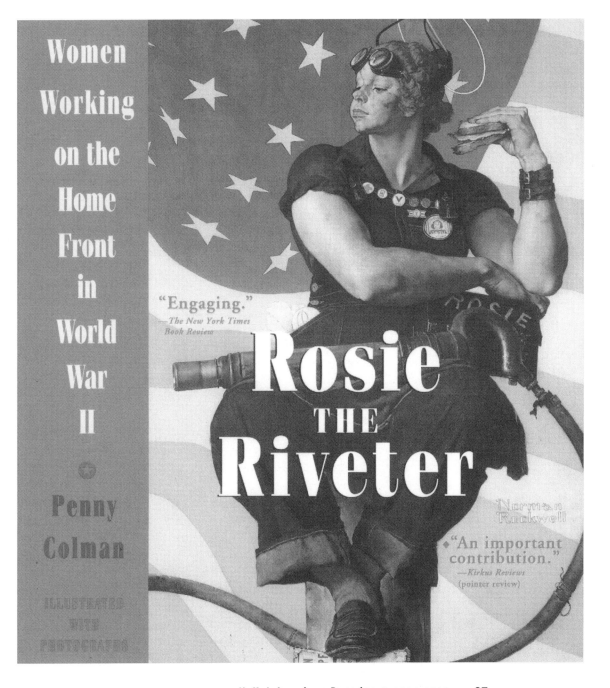

Women Working on the Home Front in World War II

Penny Colman

ILLUSTRATED WITH PHOTOGRAPHS

"Engaging."
—*The New York Times Book Review*

Rosie THE Riveter

Norman Rockwell

"An important contribution."
—*Kirkus Reviews* (pointer review)

Youth Culture

Youth culture blossomed in the "Roaring Twenties," but went into decline during the hardships of the Great Depression. It reemerged after 1945, when parents and teenagers had more money to spend on recreation. Postwar teenagers had more freedom than their predecessors, but the amount of freedom they had varied with social class. Poor black teenagers in the South had more freedom in their social lives, especially with regard to sex, than black adolescents from wealthier homes. Teenagers who had dropped out of high school were able to meet in dance halls, bowling alleys, and skating rinks. They were more sexually active than high school students. Even so, dating was an important part of the high school student's social life and was governed by a complex set of rules. Adults tried to control the way teenagers behaved on dates, especially their sexual activity. One manual for teenagers recommended topics of conversation for a date. It included the suggestion "Talk about animals: 'My dog has fleas - what'll I do?'"

did not recognize their fathers when they returned from overseas. Older children often left school early to go to work in factories, while labor laws were relaxed during the war to allow minors to go to work. A U.S. Census Bureau survey in 1944 found that one-fifth of all boys aged fourteen and fifteen were gainfully employed. A third of American girls between the ages sixteen and eighteen also had jobs. Most of these children managed to combine factory work with schooling. The traditional American family had changed forever.

For men returning from the war, the idea of their wives or girlfriends going out to work was often difficult to handle. Many had married just before going off to fight, and they had spent their time in the military dreaming of a return to traditional family life. Some had suffered physical and psychological trauma on the battlefield and found civilian life difficult. In 1946 the Veterans' Administration hospitals treated almost twenty thousand veterans for psychiatric problems. Many more were treated in regular hospitals or suffered without help. Veterans often found that returning to work in large, impersonal corporations was in many ways similar to serving in the army. But for most men, there was little opportunity for self-fulfillment at work. In the late 1940s, the family seemed to be the only area where male authority remained in place. Yet even there, traditional gender roles had begun to change. Middle-class women, who were less likely to go out to work, were better able than others to affirm the importance of their husbands' role as "breadwinner."

❖ WAR TRIGGERS RELIGIOUS REVIVAL

During the Great Depression church attendance in the United States fell steadily. In 1939, only about 43 percent of Americans were regular churchgoers. At the end of World War II in 1945, however, American churches saw a dramatic rise in their membership. By 1950, 55 percent of Americans belonged to a religious group. Between 1945 and 1949, three hundred thousand new members joined the Baptist congregation, while the Catholic Church baptized one million new babies every year. The reasons for the religious revival were complex. The experience of war left many Americans searching for some meaning to life. But the growing affluence of American society also led to social pressures. Going to church was often seen as a sign that one was a trustworthy member of the community.

The war caused problems for churches and religious leaders. Many clergymen signed up for military service, often combining their duties as chaplain with counseling of troops to help them through the ordeal of battle. At home, clergy put a huge effort into providing aid and comfort to families whose loved ones had gone off to war. Jewish Rabbi Stephen Wise (1874–1949) and Christian theologian Reinhold Niebuhr (1892–1971) advised government officials regarding decisions of life and death. At a time when God seemed to have left humanity to destroy itself, the faith and advice of such religious leaders helped sustain the nation's courage.

Not all clergy were in favor of the war, however. Pacifist A.J. Muste (1885–1967) believed there was no justification for the violence and destructiveness of war. Muste led a small group of pacifists who believed in nonviolent methods of solving the world's problems. Pacifists never gained large-scale support, but most religious groups did become more tolerant and liberal in the postwar years. Even Protestant revivalists, led by Billy Graham (1918–) in 1949, preached tolerance and humility. Although Graham's anticommunist views placed him in the politically conservative camp, his approach was more accepting of others' beliefs than it might have been a decade earlier.

There were three major religious groups in the United States in the 1940s. By the end of the decade the Catholic Church had twenty-five million communicants (active members), primarily centered in the Northeast. Catholics nationwide were far outnumbered by Protestants, however.

Put together, the Protestant churches were the dominant religious organizations in America during the 1940s. The largest single Protestant church, the Methodists, had eight million members and an annual budget of $200 million. The second-largest Protestant church was the Southern Baptist Convention, with six million members. The third major religious faith in the United States was Judaism. The five million American Jews divided themselves into three branches: Orthodox, Conservative, and Reform. Of the nations directly involved in fighting World War II, only the United States saw membership in its religious groups grow when the war ended.

Although religious observance grew after 1945, the nation's newly found affluence presented a challenge to churches and their leaders. For many people in the suburbs, going to church was a lifestyle choice rather than a sign of religious belief. Church attendance marked a person as a non-communist and someone who could be trusted to conform. As Americans moved to the new suburbs, many found themselves living next door to people of different faiths. Religious leaders such as H. Richard Niebuhr, brother of theologian Reinhold Niebuhr, worried that American religions were merging as people borrowed from one another's rituals and beliefs. During the postwar years, there was an unprecedented growth in religious activity and in tolerance between faiths. Religious groups become less distinctive and, some thought, less relevant to modern American life.

❖ AMERICANS MOVE OUT OF TOWN

As the economy expanded after 1945, more people could afford to buy their own homes. More importantly, the GI Bill gave veterans access to low-interest housing loans. But the available supply of good-quality housing was not enough to meet postwar demand. Developers such as Abraham Levitt (1880–1960) and his son, William Levitt (1907–1994), began building housing on the outskirts of cities. Levitt's simple, low-cost houses were built on vast land tracts, which soon became known as Levittown. During the second half of the 1940s, there was a record-breaking boom in house building and the arrival of suburban living on a huge scale in America.

Most of the new homes built in the 1940s were located in suburbs. For middle-class white families, a suburban home with its picture window, small plot of land, and quiet location offered the good life promised by the American dream. By 1946, for the first time, most Americans lived in houses that they owned. Suburban houses were comfortable and self-contained. Designed for mothers to stay at home to look after their children, these houses were far away from dangerous urban streets. New household appliances, such as washing machines and vacuum cleaners, made it easier to deal with the housework. The backyard was ideal for hosting barbecues and other social activities. But for some Americans, suburban living was an impossible

OPPOSITE PAGE
Jewish prisoners, waving and cheering the arrival of American liberators, Dachau, Germany, in 1945.

dream. Until 1948, the Federal Housing Authority (FHA) refused to finance houses for black families. Even when the FHA rule was found to be unconstitutional, blacks were still kept out of suburbia. It was almost impossible for African Americans to save enough money to buy a home. And even when they could, they were often unwelcome in white suburban neighborhoods.

Automania

Developments in automobiles were largely halted by World War II. But the war led to new technologies and designs that were incorporated into the American automobile of the late 1940s. Improvements to the V-8 engine, developed in the 1930s, allowed American cars to have accessories like power brakes and power steering, electrically operated windows, and air conditioning. In 1946, Buick declared that it aimed "to make those Buicks the returning warriors have dreamed about.... " Postwar cars were wider, lower, and more comfortable to ride in. Innovations such as convertibles with detachable steel roofs, better-organized instrument panels, and sleek shapes made new cars desirable to residents of the expanding suburbs. Cars also became more affordable. The cheapest, no-frills European imports, such as the British Ford, cost $1,570. American Ford offered Lincoln models priced from $2,500 up to $4,800 for the top-of-the-line Continental. Suburban life was impossible without an automobile, so as the suburbs grew, car sales also exploded. In 1945, there were 25.8 million cars registered in the United States. Between 1946 and 1950, 21.4 million new cars arrived on American roads.

The demand for suburban comforts and the scale of suburban growth were astonishing. In 1944, construction on 114,000 new houses was begun in the United States. By 1950, the number of yearly housing starts had reached a peak of 1,692,000. In some cases, people slept outside developers' offices to make sure to get the house they wanted. In early 1949, the developer Abraham Levitt (1880–1960) wrote to veterans who had applied for his $7,999 Levitt houses. The first 350 people in line on Monday, March 7, would get a home for a $90 down payment and $58 a month. Veterans began showing up outside Levitt's office on Friday night, March 4. Over the weekend, police had to control thousands of ex-GIs desperate for a new home. Levitt estimated that he could have sold at least 2,000 houses.

Suburban life had a dramatic effect on American families and their spending patterns. In the years after the war, couples began to marry and have children at younger ages than before. They competed with their suburban neighbors to obtain the latest household appliances, the right car, and invitations to social events. This competition was seen as an investment in family life rather than as greed or conspicuous consumption. But there is no doubt that the pressure to conform to the consumer culture was very strong. The expansion of the suburbs, and the demand for consumer goods it triggered, was a major factor in the economic boom that followed World War II.

❖ AFRICAN AMERICANS EXPECT MORE

In the 1940s, race relations in the United States went through a period of confusion and transition. On the one hand, after Pearl Harbor, Japanese Americans were subjected to racist taunts and ill treatment. Japanese American citizens on the West Coast were held in internment camps, and their property was sold off at below-market prices. Yet at the same time, African Americans experienced a gradual improvement in their situation. Executive Order 8802, signed by President Franklin D. Roosevelt on June 25, 1941, banned racial discrimination in the defense industries and in the federal government. It also set up the Fair Employment Practice Committee (FEPC) to investigate discrimination. Roosevelt's order was the first positive step by the federal government to ensure equal treatment for blacks and whites in the workplace.

Japanese Americans were unjustly held in internment camps in the United States during World War II. The government only recently apologized for these gross civil rights violations. **Courtesy of the National Archives and Records Administration.**

Most African Americans in the defense industries worked in low-skilled jobs. But the number in semiskilled and skilled positions began to rise. Many moved north to work in factories and found a better standard of living. These blacks were also given a voice in politics because there were fewer restrictions on who could vote in the northern states. For example, in the South, voters were required to take a test to see if they could read the ballot. Because blacks had a lower standard of education, they were more likely to fail the test and thus be unable to vote. No such testing existed in the North. Poll taxes (a tax that gave voters the right to vote) also did not exist in the North. Because Southern blacks were among the poorest residents, they were less likely to be able to pay the poll tax, and therefore often were excluded from voting in the South.

Despite Executive Order 8802, racial tension did not disappear overnight. In the military, blacks found it almost impossible to win promotion. Though opportunities improved during World War II, blacks and whites were kept apart (segregated) on many military bases. White and black soldiers often had conflicts. In cities, where many black and white workers were working together for the first time, violence erupted. In June 1943, black and white youths clashed in Detroit. As many as five thousand people rioted over three days. Twenty-five blacks and nine whites were killed, and more than seven hundred people were injured. The 1943 Detroit riot remains one of the worst race riots in American history.

The discovery of Nazi atrocities against minority groups in the early 1940s prompted a rethinking of American attitudes toward race. As the economy boomed after 1945, African Americans resented their exclusion from many postwar jobs and the lower pay they still received. Many whites agreed with them. Roosevelt's FEPC did not become a permanent commission after 1945. But on December 5, 1946, President Harry S Truman established the President's Committee on Civil Rights. On February 2, 1948, Truman delivered the first-ever presidential civil rights address to Congress. Southern Democrats blocked the passage of legislation to ban poll taxes, set up a federal antilynching law, and make the FEPC permanent. But Truman's committee paved the way for the civil rights struggles and victories of the 1950s and 1960s.

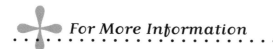

For More Information

BOOKS

Baker, Patricia. *Fashions of a Decade: The 1940s.* New York: Facts on File, 1992.

Buchanan, A. Russell. *Black Americans in World War II.* Santa Barbara, CA: Clio, 1977.

Chronicle of the Twentieth Century. Mount Cisco, NY: Chronicle, 1994.

Collier, Christopher, and James Lincoln Collier. *The United States in the Cold War.* New York: Benchmark Books/Marshall Cavendish, 2001.

Cook, Chris, and David Waller, eds. *The Longman Handbook of Modern American History, 1763–1996.* New York: Longman, 1998.

Diggins, John P. *The Proud Decades: America in War and in Peace, 1941–1960.* New York: Norton, 1988.

Harris, Cyril M. *American Architecture: An Illustrated Encyclopedia.* New York: Norton, 1998.

Heal, Edith. *The Teen-Age Manual: A Guide to Popularity and Success.* New York: Simon and Schuster, 1948.

Hunt, Marsha. *The Way We Wore: Styles of the 1930s and '40s and Our World Since Then.* Fallbrook, CA: Fallbrook, 1993.

Isaacs, Sally Senzell. *America in the Time of Franklin Delano Roosevelt: The Story of Our Nation from Coast to Coast, from 1929 to 1948.* Des Plaines, IL: Heinemann Library, 2000.

Keylin, Arleen, and Jonathan Cohen, eds. *The Forties.* New York: Arno Press, 1980.

Martin, Richard. *Jocks and Nerds: Men's Style in the Twentieth Century.* New York: Rizzoli, 1989.

May, Elaine Tyler. *Homeward Bound: American Families in the Cold War Era.* New York: Basic Books, 1988.

Melton, J. Gordon. *American Religions: An Illustrated History.* Santa Barbara, CA: ABC-CLIO, 2000.

Moloney, James H. *Encyclopedia of American Cars, 1930–1942.* Glen Ellyn, IL: Crestline, 1977.

Olian, JoAnne. *Everyday Fashions of the Forties as Pictured in Sears Catalogs.* New York: Dover Publications, 1992.

Packard, Robert T., and Balthazar Korab. *Encyclopedia of American Architecture.* New York: McGraw-Hill, 1995.

Reynolds, Helen. *The 40s & 50s: Utility to New Look.* Milwaukee, WI: Gareth Stevens, 2000.

Rollin, Lucy. *Twentieth-Century Teen Culture by the Decades: A Reference Guide.* Greenwood Press. Westport, CT: 1999.

Sicherman, Barbara, and Carol Hurd Green, editors. *Notable American Women: The Modern Period, a Biographical Dictionary.* Cambridge, MA: Harvard University Press, 1980.

Terkel, Studs. *The Good War: An Oral History of World War Two.* New York: Pantheon Books, 1984.

Willson, Quentin. *Classic American Cars.* New York: Dorling Kindersley, 1997.

Wood, Tim, and R.J. Unstead. *The 1940s.* New York: Franklin Watts, 1990.

WEB SITES

Great Buildings Online. [Online] http://www.greatbuildings.com (accessed March, 2002).

Hales, Peter Bacon. Levittown: Documents of an Ideal American Suburb. [Online] http://tigger.uic.edu/~pbhales/Levittown.html (accessed March, 2002).

National Archives and Records Administration. Powers of Persuasion: Poster Art from World War II. [Online] http://www.nara.gov/exhall/powers/powers. html (accessed March, 2002).

chapter six **Medicine and Health**

Chronology

1940: **August 28** The National Foundation for Infantile Paralysis sends aid to Indiana, where there is a massive poliomyelitis (polio) outbreak.

1940: **December** An influenza epidemic begins in California and spreads to Oregon, Washington State, New Mexico, Arizona, and Idaho.

1941: Clinical trials of penicillin begin.

1941: **March 25** The most serious measles epidemic in years breaks out along the East Coast and begins to spread westward across America.

1941: **March 27** Residents of New York are offered preventive medical care and treatment for $24 a year by the non-profit organization Group Health Association, Inc.

1941: **May 5** After successful trials, penicillin is unveiled to the public.

1941: **September** A nationwide polio epidemic kills eighty-seven people.

1942: The American Red Cross begins collecting blood to help battlefield casualties.

1942: The Kenny method of treating polio by massage is hotly disputed within the medical profession.

1942: **June** Promising progress is made toward developing a vaccine against whooping cough.

1942: **October 16** In Georgia, health officials call for all victims of sexually transmitted diseases to be kept in isolation.

1943: The antibiotic streptomycin is discovered.

1943: **July** A polio epidemic spreads through Texas, California, Washington State, Kansas, and New York.

1943: **September 8** The American Chemical Society announces the discovery of "Penicillin B." The new drug is ten times more powerful than standard penicillin.

1943: **November 3** The U.S. Census Bureau announces that 163,400 Americans died from cancer in 1942.

1943: **November 25** The Schenley Distillers Corporation develops a new and more efficient method of making penicillin.

1944: **March 3** The drug Benzedrene, a prescription amphetamine, is used by military pilots to keep them awake on long missions.

1944: **June 15** The American Medical Association (AMA) files a report criticizing the Kenny massage method of treating polio.

1944: **August 26** The New York State Hospital Commission announces the success of electroshock treatments in helping mental patients to lead normal lives.

1945: February Penicillin that can be taken orally is introduced.

1945: March 23 The U.S. Census Bureau announces that twice as many Americans have died of cancer in 1944 as in the year 1900.

1945: May 23 Typhus patients are treated successfully with streptomycin for the first time.

1945: December 16 A new sulfa drug, metachloride, proves successful in treating malaria.

1946: The American Academy of Dental Medicine is founded.

1946: The first synthetic penicillin is produced.

1946: August 9 The U.S. Public Health Service announces that the country is in the grip of the worst polio epidemic since 1916.

1946: October 27 Reported cases of syphilis increased by 42 percent in the twelve months ending June 30, 1946.

1947: February 10 In a poll for the Planned Parenthood Federation, 97.8 percent of American doctors say they are in favor of birth control.

1947: March 18 Children born in the aftermath of the atomic bombings in Hiroshima and Nagasaki, Japan, have an unusually high number of abnormalities, according to a report by the Atomic Bomb Casualties Commission.

1947: July 19 The University of Illinois announces that it will soon begin the first large-scale production of BCG, a vaccine for tuberculosis.

1947: October 3 The American Association of Science Workers states that bacteriological warfare is now the world's most important terror weapon.

1948: May 3 At the University of Minnesota, the polio virus is isolated in concentrated form for the first time.

1948: August 10 The American Cancer Society announces that $3.5 million will be spent on cancer research in the coming year.

1948: October 18 In New York City, an experiment begins to see if fluoride prevents tooth decay. Fifty thousand children have their teeth coated with sodium fluoride.

1948: December 20 Five nuclear scientists are found to be going blind because of their work with radioactive materials.

1949: February 27 The American Cancer Society and the National Cancer Institute issue a report linking smoking with lung cancer.

1949: August 12 The U.S. Public Health Service announces that the average life span of Americans has risen to 66.8 years, up from 65 years in 1939.

Overview

Many changes took place in American medicine and public health during the 1940s. The urgency of war meant that medical research was better coordinated, better financed, and better able to produce new drugs and treatments. Penicillin and "sulfa" drugs became more widely available to treat infectious diseases. The insecticide DDT destroyed insects that carried malaria and yellow fever. Better blood transfusion methods improved the speed and success of surgical operations, while technology from the nuclear industry brought new radiation therapies to fight disease. Advances in the treatment of mental health problems also were made during the decade. Many soldiers suffered mental problems as a result of combat; consequently, psychiatry (the branch of medicine concerned with mental health) took on a higher profile. Despite concerns about some of the more radical mental health treatments, psychiatric patients were treated better overall than they ever had been before.

As the decade began, the federal government took a more active role in medicine. Federal support for medical research increased, while new agencies took charge of health care and research. The National Heart Institute, the National Institute of Mental Health, and the Centers for Disease Control were all set up in the 1940s. The American Medical Association (AMA) did not like federal interference in medicine. It fought hard against calls for a national health insurance program. President Franklin D. Roosevelt and his successor, Harry S Truman, tried and failed to push the idea through Congress. But the 1946 Hospital Survey and Construction Act (known as the Hill-Burton Act) did give the federal government more freedom to pay for hospital buildings. Over 280 new hospitals were built in America during the 1940s.

The expansion of medicine was desperately needed in America. The war meant that many doctors signed up for military service, creating severe shortages of physicans across the country. Even though new hospitals were being built, medical schools did not expand enrollment to meet the increased demand for physicians. One effect of the crisis was to make health care much more expensive. The average income for physicians (before deductions for expenses) more than doubled during the 1940s, to $19,710. In the same period, the nation's total medical expenses rose from $3 billion to over $8 billion. In 1944, a middle-class American family with an annual income of $2,378 spent $148, or 6 percent of their income, on health care. Poorer families spent an even higher percentage of their income on medical expenses. Families that earned $500 a year spent about $62, or 12 percent, of their income on health care.

Overall, the health of the nation improved in the 1940s. The number of infant deaths fell as infections became easier to treat. The number of people aged sixty-five and over increased from 6.9 percent of the population to 8.2 percent. As a result, diseases of the elderly, such as cancer, heart disease, and strokes, became more common. Many infectious diseases, such as syphilis, could be treated with the new drug penicillin. But poliomyelitis (also known as infantile paralysis or polio) continued to be a problem. The polio epidemic of 1949 claimed thirty thousand victims. Yet despite such ongoing battles, for most Americans the fight against disease symbolized the nation's postwar success. Medical progress, it seemed, was unstoppable.

Alfred Blalock (1899–1964) Surgeon Alfred Blalock, along with Helen Taussig, developed the operation that saved blue babies, or babies suffering from cyanosis, a bluish coloration of the skin resulting from incomplete oxygenation of the blood. The procedure was tested on some two hundred dogs before it was performed on a baby, which occurred in 1944. Although the first baby died nine days after surgery, a success rate of 80 percent in his first 65 operations was a great success. *Photo reproduced by permission of the Corbis Corporation.*

Charles R. Drew (1904–1950) Charles R. Drew earned degrees from Amherst College in Massachusetts and McGill Medical College in Montreal, Canada. In 1939, Drew began researching blood plasma while working at Howard University. His efforts solved many problems of blood storage and made large-scale blood transfusion programs possible. He headed the American Red Cross's "Blood For Britain" campaign during 1941. Drew's research saved many lives during World War II (1939–45). Yet as an African American, he often suffered discrimination. His enemies believed that his position at the American Red Cross was too high for a black man. *Photo reproduced by permission of AP/Wide World Photos.*

Elizabeth Kenny (1886–1952) Elizabeth Kenny was a nurse in the Australian bush when she began to treat victims of polio. She tried to stop the disease from paralyzing leg and arm muscles by massaging them and encouraging exercise. She arrived in Minneapolis in 1940, but the medical profession had difficulty accepting her methods. At the time, polio victims were strapped into braces and metal frames. Kenny argued that this allowed healthy nerves and muscles to weaken. By 1950, her methods of rehabilitation were an accepted part of the treatment for polio and other muscle-wasting diseases. *Photo courtesy of the Library of Congress.*

Mary Lasker (1900–1994) Mary Lasker was the founder of the Albert and Mary Lasker Foundation. The foundation promotes the belief that scientific investigation and a fundamental understanding of human biology and disease processes are key to reducing human suffering from disease. The Foundation was established in 1942 with a mission that was novel at the time: to encourage federal financial support for biomedical research in the United States. The belief was that the foundation should provide seed money for research projects, then stimulate the federal government to continue the efforts. The foundation also created a venue for educating the public about the many benefits of research for human health. *Photo reprodeuced by permission of AP/Wide World Photos.*

William Claire Menninger (1899–1966) At a time when psychiatry (the treatment of mental health problems) was not taken seriously in the United States, William Claire Menninger worked hard to improve the treatment of the mentally ill. He persuaded the army to take better care of its mentally injured soldiers, and he improved psychiatry after the war. Menniger's great triumph was persuading doctors and the public that mental problems could be treated. He received the Albert Lasker Award in 1944 for "outstanding service in the field of mental hygiene." *Photo reproduced by permission of the Corbis Corporation.*

B. F. Skinner (1904–1990) Behavioral psychology explains that all learning and behavior are a direct result of external stimulation. For B. F. Skinner, "human nature" did not exist. Instead, he believed that human behavior could be influenced and changed. Always a controversial figure, Skinner was criticized for taking away free will. But his techniques have found great success in anti-addiction clinics. By the late 1940s, he had become one of the most influential American psychologists. *Photo courtesy of the Library of Congress.*

Henry Stack Sullivan (1892–1949) Henry Stack Sullivan believed that personality disorders are caused by the relationship between the patient and the environment. Mental illness, he thought, was a problem-solving technique used by the mind to deal with difficult situations. Working as medical adviser to the War Department, Sullivan helped raise the profile of mental health treatment in the army as well as in civilian medicine. In particular, he persuaded the medical profession that schizophrenia was a curable condition. Rather than just trying to understand the problem, Sullivan made the therapist an important part of the patient's recovery. *Photo courtesy of the Library of Congress.*

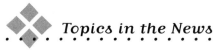

Topics in the News

❖ AMERICA GOES TO WAR AGAINST DISEASE

An epidemic is defined as the rapid spread of a disease through a population. Epidemics are very dangerous because they affect large numbers of people and give medical and governmental authorities very little time to react. Once an epidemic has begun, it is often very difficult to bring it under control. In the 1940s, several diseases threatened to become epidemics including influenza, polio, malaria, typhus, dengue fever, and yellow fever. When American military personnel returned from abroad, many of them brought back contagious illnesses such as typhus and malaria, thus putting their colleagues and fellow citizens at risk.

The Office of Malaria Control in War Areas (MCWA) was an emergency organization based in Atlanta, Georgia during World War II (1939–45). Although originally set up to tackle malaria, a serious threat in the Atlanta area, in 1943 it expanded to deal with dengue fever in Hawaii and yellow fever in the southeastern states. In 1945, the MCWA used specially trained teams of scientists to find out the main causes of infectious diseases. In 1946, it was reorganized for peacetime by U.S. Surgeon General Thomas Parran (1892–1968), and it was renamed the Communicable Disease Center. Later known as the Centers for Disease Control and Prevention (CDC), the agency tries to manage and control diseases spread from person to person, from animal to person, and from the environment. One of the most powerful weapons it had against disease during the 1940s was the insecticide DDT.

DDT (or dichlorodiphenyltrichloroethane) was first made in 1874, and its ability to kill insects was discovered in the 1930s. One advantage of using DDT as an insecticide was that it stayed active for many months after it was used. DDT sprayed on a mattress would remain toxic to bed bugs for almost a year. Clothing dusted with the chemical stayed free of lice for up to a month, even when it was regularly washed. This was especially important for military personnel, since many soldiers caught typhus from lice. DDT also controlled the spread of malaria. Just a few ounces of DDT dropped in a swamp killed all the mosquito larvae, thereby stopping the spread of malaria by mosquito bite.

Around 350,000 pounds of DDT were manufactured every month in the late 1940s. The insecticide was used in the home, on the battlefield, and on farm crops to protect them from worms, moths, and aphids. Scientists insisted DDT was safe for humans as long as they did not eat it. But it would be twenty years before the negative effects of DDT were recognized. The most important of these was the way it destroyed all insects, leaving no food for birds, small mammals, and other important creatures. The effect of using DDT was to destroy all wildlife, causing a "silent spring," the term used later by environmental activist and author Rachel Carson.

Federal support for disease control expanded rapidly in the 1940s. Apart from advising on where chemicals such as DDT should be used, the CDC was responsible for much of the research into the spread of disease. Not only did its scientists work on the biology of diseases, but they also plotted epidemics using statistics. In this way, they learned a great deal about the way epidemics worked and how to control them.

❖ MEDICAL SCHOOLS REJECT MINORITY STUDENTS

As the 1940s began, there was already a severe shortage of doctors in the United States. When America joined the war in December 1941, many younger doctors enlisted and were sent abroad. In a period of just three years, the patient-to-doctor ratio more than doubled, to 1,700 to 1. Yet despite severe physician shortages, well-qualified members of ethnic minority groups such as Jews, Italians, and African Americans found it difficult to find a place at medical colleges.

DDT was widely used to kill bugs that could infect soldiers during World War II. Later it was discovered that DDT had extremely harmful effects on the environment and living organisms. **Courtesy of the Library of Congress.**

Medical Fads of the 1940s

Advances in medicine in the 1940s gave many doctors the hope that, in the long run, most human ailments would be curable. But they often found problems where none existed. In New York in 1945, for example, 61 percent of eleven-year-olds had already had their tonsils removed, and doctors believed that around half of the rest would benefit from a preventive tonsillectomy (an operation to remove the tonsils). By the end of the century, conventional medical practice was not to remove tonsils except in extreme cases of infection. Other minor symptoms diagnosed as serious ailments during the 1940s were flat feet, crooked teeth, poor posture, and heart murmurs. None of these are considered serious problems today.

One reason given for this difficulty was overcrowding. There were eight applicants for every freshman vacancy. But minority students found they were more likely to be passed over for admission than white students. It is estimated that between 35 and 50 percent of applicants to medical schools in the 1940s were Jewish. Yet only one in thirteen Jewish applicants was accepted. For African Americans the situation was even more desperate. One-third of the seventy-eight approved medical schools were in the southern and border states. All twenty-six of those colleges were closed to black students. There were just two black medical schools in the 1940s: Howard and Meharry. The others ran hidden quota systems for minority applicants, admitting a small fixed number of black, Italian, Catholic, and women students.

A way around discrimination in U.S. medical schools was to study abroad. Before the war, many affluent Jewish and African American students studied medicine in England, Scotland, and elsewhere. After 1945, however, the National Board of Medical Examiners would not allow graduates of foreign medical schools to take its examinations to practice medicine in the United States. Only English schools were exempt. This restriction not only stopped many Americans from studying abroad, but it also prevented immigrant doctors from practicing medicine. Despite the shortage of homegrown doctors, and the large numbers of European immigrants, there were almost no foreign-born doctors on hospital staffs in the 1940s. Yet medical schools denied that they were racist. They claimed their quota systems were based on geographical and income distribution rather than on race. After fighting the Nazis, many Americans wanted to see racism removed from daily life. Even so, official and unofficial quota systems would remain part of American medicine for many years to come.

❖ PRESIDENT TRUMAN TAKES ON THE AMA

The issue of whether or not the United States should have a compulsory health insurance system was brought to a head in the late 1940s. Many European nations, including Germany, had set up similar systems up to fifty years before. American attempts to create some form of national health insurance plan first began in 1915. That year, the American Association for Labor Legislation proposed medical protection for workers and their families. Throughout his period as president of the United States, beginning in 1933, Franklin D. Roosevelt was keen on developing a national health-care system. In 1945, a few months after the war ended, his successor, Harry S Truman, asked Congress to pass a national medical care program.

Truman's health-care bill went before Congress on November 19, 1945. The plan included federal funding to build new hospitals, to expand public health and disease prevention measures, and to create more medical schools, compulsory health insurance, and disability insurance. The American Medical Association (AMA) could not argue with the need for more medical schools or additional public health measures. But it was deeply opposed to compulsory insurance. The AMA was especially unhappy because the insurance Truman had in mind would cover all classes of society, not just the needy. This would remove the freedom of doctors to set their own fees.

Despite a lukewarm response from Congress, the American public favored the proposed system at first. It would remove much of the "economic fear" associated with being sick. But the AMA and Republicans in Congress fought hard against Truman's plans. Senator Robert Taft (1889–1953) of Ohio attacked it as creeping socialism. He said: "It is to my mind the most socialistic measure this Congress has ever had before it." The Republicans took control of Congress in 1946, and Truman's bill foundered. But after his surprise presidential election victory in 1948, Truman kept up the pressure. The AMA spent $1.5 million fighting national health insurance in the 1940s. At the time, it was the most expensive political lobbying in history.

In the end, the AMA succeeded in killing off Truman's plans for national health insurance. They did so by appealing to the nation in the language of the cold war. National health insurance, the AMA argued, was the first step toward becoming a socialist state like the Soviet Union. In the tense political atmosphere of the late 1940s, many Americans were convinced by the AMA's warnings. Public support disappeared, and the idea of a national health-insurance program was shelved. It was defeated by the wealth and power of the AMA, which was supported by businesses trying to avoid the extra costs mandatory health insurance would impose on them. The episode was an example of the way big business and powerful lobbying groups could directly influence American government policy.

❖ "MAGIC BULLETS" USED TO FIGHT INFECTIOUS DISEASES

As in other areas of technology, World War II also speeded up discoveries in medicine. Many breakthroughs in drug treatments for infectious diseases had been made in the 1930s. But it was in the 1940s that those medicines came into common use. Antibiotics, or drugs that combat bacterial infections, were widely used in the 1940s. They saved many lives on the battlefields of Asia and Europe, and they revolutionized the treatment of illness in the second half of the twentieth century. Such drug treatments were known as "magic bullets" because they could kill many different infectious diseases.

The first real breakthrough in the war against infectious disease came in 1932. In that year, German chemist Gerhard Domagk (1895–1964) discovered that a red dye known as Protosil protected mice against the streptococcal infection. In 1936, the active ingredient in the dye, sulfanilamide, was identified. A whole series of "sulfa" drugs were developed as war broke out in Europe. By the early 1940s, these sulfa drugs were in use around the world. U.S. and Australian troops used the sulfa drug sulfaguanidine to treat dysentery contracted by soldiers in New Guinea. Their common foe, the Japanese army, suffered from the same illness but was soon beaten because of an inability to treat it. Sulfa drugs also could treat streptococcal infections, pneumonia, gonorrhea, meningitis, and many other diseases.

Sulfa drugs quickly became part of every physician's prescription arsenal. But other drugs were also becoming available. Although Scottish scientist Alexander Fleming (1881–1955) first discovered penicillin in 1928, drug companies did not take an interest until 1941. That year, when American scientists discovered a faster-growing type of penicillin on a rotten cantaloupe melon, penicillin soon went into industrial production. By 1942, there was enough penicillin on Earth to treat around one hundred patients. By 1943, with the U.S. government in charge of penicillin production, the United States was able to supply the entire needs of the Allied armed forces. Penicillin was especially useful to the military. Before antibiotics like penicillin came along, many soldiers with minor wounds died of

In 1946, it was estimated that up to 20 million Americans suffered allergic reactions of one kind or another. There was no relief for symptoms such as itchiness, swelling, sneezing, and skin rashes. Sufferers simply had to avoid whatever it was that affected them. Then, in 1946, scientists discovered histamine, the chemical in the body that causes allergic reactions. Not long afterward, they invented a drug to stop the effects of histamine. The new antihistamine drug was effective in 85 percent of hay fever sufferers, and in 50 percent of allergic asthma patients. The chemical name of the antihistamine was beta-dimethylaminoethyl benzhydryl ether hydrochloride. Fortunately, someone came up with a shorter name: Benadryl.

infections. This was also true after surgery, in both military and civilian medicine. Many patients who survived operations died a few days later from infected wounds. Penicillin went into civilian use in 1945.

Other antibiotics besides penicillin were also discovered or developed in the 1940s. Selman A. Waksman (1888–1973), who studied tiny organisms living in soil, discovered actinomycin, an antibiotic taken from a type of fungus. Actinomycin turned out to be toxic to humans, but Waksman's research also led to the discovery of streptomycin. This antibiotic is effective against bacteria untouched by penicillin. It effectively removed the threat of killer diseases such as tuberculosis. Soil scientists also discovered chloromycetin, an antibiotic that cures a whole range of diseases, including typhus. It was developed from a substance found in soil in Venezuela; chloromycetin went into general use in 1949.

These so-called magic bullets changed medicine dramatically. Within a few years, diseases that were thought to be untreatable could be cured. Though some antibiotics had toxic effects, they increased people's expectation of a long and healthy life. But the magic bullets were not perfect; even in the 1940s, there were signs that some infectious diseases were becoming resistant to sulfa drugs. And doctors slowly learned that patients can be left even more vulnerable to disease if they do not complete a prescribed course of antibiotics. Since the 1940s, many antibiotics, including penicillin, have lost their power to combat certain strains of infectious disease.

Common Killers

. . . .

During World War II, 325,000 Americans were killed by enemy action. But in 1945 the U.S. Census Bureau reported that between 1942 and 1944, around 500,000 people were killed by cancer. In the first half of the decade, 2 million Americans died from diseases of the heart and blood vessels. Heart disease was the number-one killer illness in the 1940s. Yet Americans did not rate it as a major threat. In April 1940, a Gallup poll showed that the four diseases Americans believed to pose the biggest risk to public health were: syphilis (46 percent); cancer (29 percent); tuberculosis (16 percent); and infantile paralysis, or polio (9 percent).

❖ WAR ADVANCES MEDICINE

During the 1930s, President Franklin D. Roosevelt offered federal support for health care through his New Deal policies. But World War II had a much greater impact on the development of medicine in the United States. Increased government funding for research brought advances in drug therapies, surgery, and disease prevention. The federal government even helped with the manufacture and distribution of new medicines. The problems faced by soldiers on the front lines led to improvements in psychiatry, as well as the treatment of physical injuries, fatigue, and exposure. Military personnel also were much more likely to suffer from diseases such as influenza, pneumonia, dysentery, gangrene, and venereal (sexually transmitted) diseases. The pressures of war greatly increased the speed and success of medical research in those areas.

But although drug treatments and medical knowledge advanced during the war years, World War II caused problems for civilian medicine. The peacetime Army Medical Corps numbered around twelve hundred medical personnel. With a wartime army of eight million soldiers, the Medical Corps had to be expanded. At its peak, it included forty-six thousand medical staff members working in fifty-two general hospital units and twenty evacuation hospital units. Most of the doctors and trained medical staff were taken from civilian hospitals. This triggered a crisis in medical care at home. In an effort to solve the shortage of doctors, medical schools cut the length of their programs from four to three years. Although the three-year courses were year-round programs rather than four nine-month periods, many doctors complained of falling quality. The Committee on Medical Research of the Office of Scientific Research and Development declared that the intensive course led to "surface learning" and poor discipline among young doctors.

The war also changed the way physicians thought about their profession and brought new branches of medicine into the mainstream. In civilian life, most doctors worked on their own or in small private practices. Wartime experience taught them the value of group practice. It allowed individual physicians to develop special interests and skills that could benefit patients. But having experienced life in the army, many were resistant to the idea of giving up control in their civilian life. During the late 1940s, physicians and the federal government struggled for control of American medicine.

❖ STEPS TAKEN TOWARD A POLIO VACCINE

One of the most feared diseases of the 1940s was poliomyelitis (also known as infantile paralysis or polio). Parents were terrified when their children complained of headaches, fever, or sore throats. These were all symptoms of polio. Although in most cases the virus cleared up completely in a few days, a significant number of children, and some adults, were permanently affected. Of those whose nervous system was invaded by the disease, 25 percent suffered mild disability. Another 25 percent became severely disabled, with paralyzed arms and legs. In some cases, the disease paralyzed muscles in the throat and chest, stopping the patient from breathing. More children died from polio during the 1940s than from any other infectious disease. The summer months were the time when epidemics (the rapid spread of diseases) broke out. Children spread polio among themselves when they played together in swimming pools and around playgrounds. When a local polio epidemic broke out, parents kept their children indoors, away from the risk of infection.

Many scientists actually believed it was lack of exposure to the disease that was causing large outbreaks. Improved sanitation since the end of World War I meant that children could avoid contact with polio until they were able to go out on their own. By then, their natural resistance to the disease had become weak. This theory was supported by the fact that the age of polio victims was rising. In 1949, the U.S. Public Health Service published figures showing that, in 1916, 95 percent of polio victims were under the age of ten. In 1947, only 52 percent were below that age. Like President Franklin D. Roosevelt, whose legs were paralyzed by the disease at the age of thirty-nine, an increasing number of those afflicted were adults. This shift in the age distribution caused an unexpected problem for the U.S. Army. Many American soldiers had been brought up in well-kept, modern homes. When they were exposed to the polio virus in the filthy conditions of the battlefield, they caught the disease easily.

After 1945, the number of polio victims continued to rise. By 1949, there were over thirty thousand cases reported each year. But although a 1943 study had shown that gamma globulin (a substance taken from blood) protected monkeys from polio infection, it was impossible to test the technique on humans. With no known cure, polio patients had their paralyzed limbs supported with mechanical braces. If necessary, they were kept breathing with an "iron lung" machine. Elizabeth Kenny (1886–1952) treated patients by massaging their paralyzed limbs and had some success. But the medical profession was unsure of her methods and they were not widely used. The only way to be sure not to contract polio was to stay away from any known victims and to avoid swimming pools and other public places. In other words, it was impossible.

Although polio was still incurable in the 1940s, scientists were gradually winning the race to find a vaccine. John F. Enders (1897–1985), a virologist (virus expert) at Harvard University, discovered a way to artificially produce large quantities of the polio virus quickly in the laboratory. Vaccines are based on a dead or weakened strain of the virus, so large amounts are needed for mass vaccination programs to succeed. Enders's discovery made possible the production of polio vaccines by Jonas Salk (1915–1995) and Albert Sabin (1906–1993) in the 1950s. In 1954, Enders was awarded the Nobel Prize in physiology or medicine for his work on polio.

❖ MENTAL PATIENTS SHOCKED INTO SANITY

Methods of treating mental illness during the 1940s were limited. There were few drug therapies that allowed patients to live normal lives. Severe cases of depression, mania, and schizophrenia were almost untreatable. But in the late 1930s, the idea of shock therapy using drugs or electricity became popular. Early shock therapies were carried out using drugs such as insulin, camphor, or metrazol. Injections of insulin sent patients into a deep coma, while metrazol caused convulsions and spasms. Patients suffering from schizophrenia seemed to respond best to these treatments. Electric shock therapy, however, was cheaper, more easily controlled, and less dangerous than drug therapies. First developed in Italy in 1938, electroconvulsive therapy (ECT), as it was known, soon became the most common treatment for severe mental illness. In 1944, the New York Academy of Medicine produced a study that claimed that an eight-week course of electric shock therapy could replace many years of mental hospital care.

*Thousands of American
children, and later adults,
suffered from paralysis
when they contracted
polio during the 1940s.*
**Reproduced by permission of
the Corbis Corporation.**

An even more drastic treatment for mental illness was psychosurgery. Psychosurgery was first practiced in the United States in 1936 by Walter Freeman (1895–1972). By the 1940s it was an accepted treatment technique. Psychosurgery involved cutting away parts of the brain that were thought to be malfunctioning. In 1941, two hundred Americans had brain surgery for mental illnesses such as depression, suicidal tendencies, and violent episodes. Surgeons used a long, hollow needle to disconnect the front parts of the brain (known as the prefrontal lobes) from the rest. By disconnecting them, doctors hoped to make patients calmer and easier to manage.

Doctors reported that patients regained their emotional responses after a long recovery period. But they were also left confused, withdrawn, and unable to cope with social situations. In the second half of the decade, it

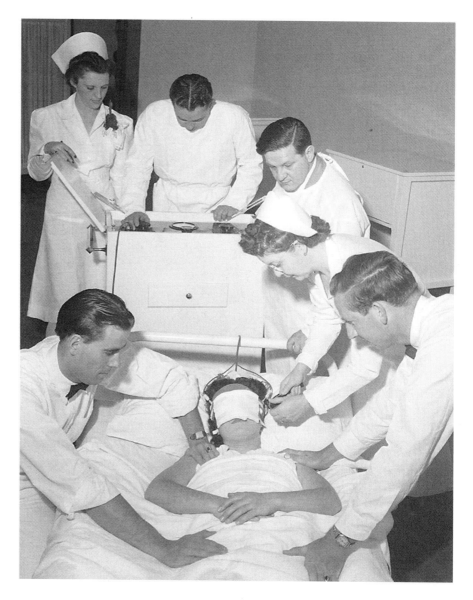

became clear that psychosurgery was being used primarily as a way to control difficult and dangerous patients. The operation could not be reversed, and many people thought the "cure" was worse than the disease. Even so, in the twenty-first century psychosurgery is still used in certain extreme cases.

Beyond the headline-grabbing stories of electric shocks and psychosurgery, the specialty of psychiatry made major steps forward during the 1940s. For the first time, the mental health of Americans came under scrutiny during World War II. Medical examinations of men drafted into

In the 1940s, clinical depression, or "melancholia," was the ailment most commonly treated using electric shocks, known as electroconvulsive therapy (ECT). The patient would be strapped to a hospital table with electrodes attached to the sides of his or her head. Patients were usually sedated because spasms caused by the shock could injure neck muscles. A current of between seventy and one hundred volts was applied to the head for one-tenth of a second. The patient was knocked unconscious by the shock but usually revived within a few minutes. This treatment was repeated three times a day for up to eight weeks. ECT was not thought to be dangerous. But it caused memory loss, confusion, and sometimes left patients with a sore neck. In the twenty-first century, ECT is still used for the treatment of severe depression, but it remains very controversial.

the military showed a surprising number with mental or neurological (brain-related) illnesses. More than 1,000,000 recruits were rejected on those grounds. The horror of war caused mental disorders in many thousands of serving soldiers. Around 850,000 men were treated for mental problems caused by the war. The 25 psychiatric specialists assigned to the Army in 1940 had expanded to 2,400 by 1944.

When the war ended, such statistics were used to persuade the government and medical organizations that psychiatry was a medical specialty worthy of support. In 1946, Congress passed the National Mental Health Act. The act put in place education programs for thousands of mental health professionals. It began a trend in psychiatry toward the prevention of mental illness. In the 1940s, for the first time, mental patients were treated as people who could be helped.

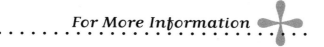

For More Information

BOOKS

Bender, Lionel. *Frontiers of Medicine*. New York: Gloucester Press, 1991.

Bordley, James, and A. McGehee Harvey. *Two Centuries of American Medicine, 1776–1976*. Philadelphia: Saunders, 1976.

Bryan, Jenny. *The History of Health and Medicine.* Austin, TX: Raintree Steck-Vaughn, 1996.

Burge, Michael C., and Don Nardo. *Vaccines: Preventing Disease.* San Diego, CA: Lucent Books, 1992.

The Cambridge World History of Human Disease. New York: Cambridge University Press, 1993.

Chronicle of the Twentieth Century. Mount Cisco, NY: Chronicle, 1994.

Cohen, Daniel. *The Last 100 Years: Medicine.* New York: M. Evans, 1981.

Companion Encyclopedia of the History of Medicine. London: Routledge, 1993.

Cook, Chris, and David Waller, eds. *The Longman Handbook of Modern American History, 1763–1996.* Harlow, NY: Longman, 1998.

Cunningham, Robert III, and Robert Cunningham Jr. *The Blues: A History of the Blue Cross and Blue Shield System.* DeKalb, IL: Northern Illinois University Press, 1997.

Duden, Jane. *1940s.* New York: Crestwood House, 1989.

Feinstein, Stephen. *The 1940s From World War II to Jackie Robinson.* Berkeley Heights, NJ: Enslow Publishers, 2000.

Garza, Hedda. *Women in Medicine.* New York: Franklin Watts, 1994.

Gordon, Karen. *Selman Waksman and the Discovery of Streptomycin.* Bear, DE: Mitchell Lane Publishers, 2002.

Hills, Ken. *1940s.* Austin, TX: Raintree Steck-Vaughn, 1992.

Landau, Elaine. *Tuberculosis.* New York: Franklin Watts, 1995.

McGrew, Roderick E. *Encyclopedia of Medical History.* New York: McGraw-Hill, 1985.

Miller, Brandon Marie. *Just What the Doctor Ordered: The History of American Medicine.* Minneapolis, MN: Lerner Publications, 1997.

Lyons, Albert S. *Medicine: An Illustrated History.* New York: Abrams, 1978.

Otfinoski, Steven. *Alexander Fleming: Conquering Disease with Penicillin.* New York: Facts on File, 1992.

Parker, Steve. *Medical Advances.* Austin, TX: Raintree Steck-Vaughn, 1998.

Press, Petra. *A Multicultural Portrait of Learning in America.* New York: Marshall Cavendish, 1994.

Royston, Angela. *100 Greatest Medical Discoveries.* Danbury, CT: Grolier Educational, 1997.

Scheehan, Angela, ed. *The Marshall Cavendish Encyclopedia of Health.* New York: Marshall Cavendish, 1995.

Senior, Kathryn. *Medicine: Doctors, Demons, and Drugs.* New York: Franklin Watts, 1993.

Silverstein, Alvin, et al. *Polio.* Berkeley Heights, NJ: Enslow Publishers, 2001.

Stille, Darlene R. *Extraordinary Women of Medicine.* New York: Children's Press, 1997.

Uschan, Michael V. *The 1940s.* San Diego, CA: Lucent Books, 1999.

Wood, Tim, and R.J. Unstead. *The 1940s.* New York: Franklin Watts, 1990.

Yount, Lisa. *History of Medicine.* San Diego, CA: Lucent Books, 2001.

WEB SITES

American Red Cross History: 1940–1959. [Online] http://www.redcross.org/museum/19401959.html (accessed March 2002).

Blue Cross and Blue Shield History. [Online] http://www.bcbs.com/whoweare/history.html (accessed March 2002).

Science and Technology

1940: **May 15** The Vought-Sikorsky corporation successfully flight-tests the first working helicopter.

1940: **June 15** President Franklin D. Roosevelt sets up the National Defense Research Committee (NDRC). Headed by Vannevar Bush, the NDRC organizes scientific research for the war.

1940: **July 8** Trans World Airlines (TWA) begins the first commercial flights using planes with pressurized cabins.

1941: The Atanasoff Berry Computer (ABC) is the first prototype digital computer. It does not work.

1941: **April** At the Massachusetts Institute of Technology (MIT), the Radiation Laboratory or "Rad Lab" develops a prototype AI-10 radar machine that can detect aircraft and submarines.

1941: **June 28** In an executive order, President Roosevelt establishes the Office of Scientific Research and Development (OSRD). It includes the earlier NDRC.

1942: Napalm is developed for use in U.S. Army flame throwers.

1942: The first American jet aircraft, the Bell P59-A is tested at Muroc Army Base in California.

1942: **June** President Roosevelt approves the Manhattan Project, a secret research program that will eventually build and explode the first atomic bomb.

1942: **December 2** On a disused squash court at the University of Chicago, physicist Enrico Fermi conducts the first controlled experimental release of nuclear energy.

1943: For the first time, radar is used to guide a plane to a landing. Physicist Luis Alvarez operates the guidance system.

1943: **December** The Harvard-IBM Mark-1 Automatic Sequence Controlled Calculator becomes the first computer to successfully follow a sequence of commands.

1944: The U.S. military goes to war against body lice on troops and civilians using the insecticide DDT.

1944: In biology, scientists find evidence that DNA is responsible for inherited genetic characteristics.

1944: **March 1** At Oak Ridge, Tennessee, the secret Manhattan Project laboratory produces a few milligrams of plutonium, the radioactive substance needed to make an atomic bomb.

1945: The Electronic Numerical Integrator and Calculator (ENIAC) becomes the first successful electronic digital computer.

1945: July 16 In the Trinity Test, the world's first atomic bomb is detonated at Alamogordo, New Mexico.

1945: August 6 The first atomic weapon used in warfare is a uranium bomb, dropped from an American Super-fortress bomber on Hiroshima, Japan. It kills over fifty thousand people.

1945: August 9 A second atomic bomb, this time made of plutonium, is dropped by an American bomber on the Japanese city of Nagasaki. Over forty thousand people are killed instantly.

1946: July 12 The technique of "cloud seeding" is pioneered by Vincent Schaefer, who uses dry ice to produce a rain shower.

1946: August 1 The U.S. Atomic Energy Com-mission (AEC) begins its job of monitor-ing and controlling nuclear power.

1947: Using a type of carbon known as car-bon-14, chemist Willard Libby develops his radiocarbon-dating method. This is the technique used to establish the age of archaeological finds, among other things.

1947: February 21 The "camera-and-film" system is invented by Edwin Land. It later goes on sale as the Polaroid Land Camera, the first camera to develop its own photographs.

1947: June Pan American Airways' *America*, a Lockheed Constellation airliner, be-comes the first aircraft to circle the globe while carrying paying passengers.

1947: October 14 The Bell X-1 rocket plane reaches a speed of seven hundred miles per hour. It is the first plane to travel faster than the speed of sound.

1948: Chemist Karl Folkers isolates Vitamin B_{12}.

1948: Peter Goldmark markets the world's first long playing record.

1948: June 3 At the Mount Palomar Obser-vatory at the California Institute of Technology, the two-hundred-inch Hale telescope is completed. It is the largest telescope ever built.

1948: November 20 A new balloon altitude record of 26.5 miles is set by the U.S. Army Signal Corps.

1949: February 24 The first rocket with more than one stage is launched.

1949: February 25 At White Sands, New Mexico, a U.S. Navy Corporal rocket sets a new rocketry altitude record of 250 miles. It also becomes the first true space vehicle.

1949: March 2 The U.S. Air Force Super-fortress B-50, known as *Lucky Lady*, completes the first nonstop flight around the world.

Overview

The pace of scientific discovery in the 1940s was staggering. World War II (1939–45) boosted research in science and technology through government funding. It led to new technologies that transformed American life after 1945. The demands of war inspired the production of new substances and materials such as the antibiotic penicillin, the insecticide DDT, and synthetic rubber. New technologies such as radar, the jet engine, helicopters, and electronic computers all were wartime innovations. With the creation of the atomic bomb, American scientists influenced the political and cultural atmosphere of the rest of the century and beyond.

Most scientists in the early 1940s were engaged in research that served military needs. The U.S. government poured millions of dollars into research projects that would help win the war. There were major advances in transportation, communication, weapons, and intelligence-gathering technologies. But government funding also brought science and politics together in a new way. For the first time, the U.S. government funded scientific research that would help it achieve its political aims. Perhaps the most important and controversial of these projects was the research on the atomic bomb.

In 1939, Austrian physicist Lise Meitner and German chemist Otto Hahn, described atoms being split into smaller atoms and releasing huge amounts of energy. The process they described was nuclear fission, the reaction that takes place inside an atomic bomb. German Jewish physicist Albert Einstein settled in the United States in 1933, after escaping from Nazi Germany. Though he had always been opposed to violence and war, his experience with the Nazis convinced him that Western democracies would have to fight to keep their freedom. After news of the fission experiments in Europe reached American scientists, Einstein was persuaded to write to President Franklin D. Roosevelt warning him of the danger. He managed to convince Roosevelt that the United States should try to develop an atomic bomb before Germany did. As a result, in 1942 Roosevelt authorized the Manhattan Project to begin research into nuclear weapons. In 1945, the United States became the world's first nuclear power.

Einstein did not contribute directly to the Manhattan Project. But he was one of a number of European scientists who emigrated to the United States in the 1930s and 1940s, and many of these scientists did help develop the atomic bomb. Physicists and chemists such as Germany's Hans Bethe, Switzerland's Felix Bloch, and Italy's Enrico Fermi and Bruno Rossi—along with others from Russia, Hungary, Poland, and Austria—all worked on the Manhattan Project.

Many other important discoveries were made by immigrant American scientists in the 1940s. George Gamows developed the "big bang" theory of the start of the universe. Research on DNA was conducted by Erwin Chargoff and Severo Ochoa. Another significant advance was the development of rocketry. Werhner von Braun, in particular, did important work on rockets during the decade that led to the space program in years to come. Many of these scientists had won Nobel Prizes for their research while in Europe. Others became Nobel laureates (prize winners) after settling in the United States. This "brain drain" of scientists from Europe to America helped make the United States the world leader in scientific research after the war.

In peacetime, scientific researchers can afford the luxury of investigating questions or problems that have no obvious practical use. This is known as "pure" science. Discoveries made in pure scientific research often find practical uses years later. During World War II, American scientists were forced to find much closer links between their research and practical problems. For example, developments in theoretical physics helped create the atomic bomb. In chemistry, synthetic rubber was the practical outcome of years of pure research. Only biologists seemed free from wartime pressures. Researchers working in the field of genetics began laying the foundations for the discovery of the structure of DNA in the 1950s. Such research had no obvious application to the war effort.

In the 1940s, American scientific research fed into practical technological advances as never before. A great deal of money was made available for research, accelerating the pace of discovery and development. Science and technology came to the fore in American colleges and universities. Before the war, the United States was already a powerful industrial nation. By the late 1940s, it led the world in scientific research as well. But the close link between political needs and scientific development changed the way scientists worked. During the war years, "pure" research lost out to applied research, or work that would provide quick solutions to practical problems. After 1945, American scientists had to rediscover the balance between "pure" and applied science.

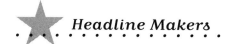

Vannevar Bush (1890–1974) As head of the Office of Scientific Research and Development (OSRD), Vannevar Bush managed the development of the atomic bomb. He always saw himself as an engineer. At the Massachusetts Institute of Technology after 1919, he invented the justifying typewriter (a typewriter that can produce documents with straight margins on both sides of the page). Another of his inventions was the differential analyzer, the most important calculating machine of its time. During the 1940s, through the OSRD, Bush helped organize American science for the war effort and made sure atomic research was controlled. He was strongly against the development of the hydrogen bomb. *Photo courtesy of the Library of Congress.*

Gerty Theresa Cori (1896–1957) The first American to receive the Nobel Prize for medicine or physiology, Gerty Theresa Cori worked with her husband on research into blood. They moved to the United States in 1922 from Czechoslovakia. The Coris worked together throughout their careers, but Gerty spent many years as a research associate on a token salary. She was given a full faculty post only when she and her husband won the Nobel Prize. Nevertheless, her work on the classification of blood diseases has since been described as "an unmatched scientific achievement." *Photo courtesy of the Library of Congress.*

Enrico Fermi (1901–1954) Winner of the Nobel Prize for physics in 1938, Enrico Fermi immigrated to the United States from Italy the same year. He joined the Manhattan Project in 1942, and by December of that year he had become the first person to conduct a controlled nuclear chain reaction. Fermi was one of four scientists who advised the government that dropping an atomic bomb on Japan was the only way to end World War II. He continued as an adviser to government on the development and use of nuclear weapons until his death.

J. Robert Oppenheimer (1904–1967) J. Robert Oppenheimer completed the four-year Harvard University degree program in just three years, graduating in 1925. He became a revered teacher at the University of California, Berkeley. In 1942, Oppenheimer joined the Manhattan Project where he was in charge of solving theoretical problems with the atomic bomb. After the first successful test on July 16, 1945, Oppenheimer quoted from the Hindu holy book, the Bhagavad Gita: "I am become death, the destroyer of worlds." In the early 1950s, he was charged with having had leftist friends in the 1930s and refused a government security clearance. In 1963, President Lyndon B. Johnson (1908–1973) awarded him the prestigious Fermi Award. *Photo reproduced by permission of Archive Photos, Inc.*

Edward Teller (1908–) Often called the "father of the hydrogen bomb," Edward Teller worked on the Manhattan Project during the 1940s. He was outspoken in his view that the United States should build the hydrogen bomb to counter the Soviet threat. Born in Budapest, Hungary, Teller immigrated to the United States in 1935. He was a key figure in the development of the first plutonium bomb, and he criticized scientists who urged caution in nuclear research. In 1954, he testified against J. Robert Oppenheimer before Congress and thereafter was largely ignored by many scientists. *Photo courtesy of the Library of Congress.*

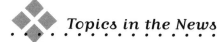

Topics in the News

❖ SCIENTISTS UNRAVEL HUMAN SOCIETIES

Before the 1940s, archaeologists spent most of their time putting the artifacts they found in chronological order. They were mostly interested in how old a found object might be relative to other objects. In the 1940s, however, they began to look at their finds in a different way. While it was still important to date an object, it became even more interesting to try to work out how it had been used. Objects from the past could help scientists learn about how people lived and how ancient societies worked.

The way archaeologists in the 1940s used objects to explain ancient societies was first to look at where an object was found (known as the microcontext), and then compare it with similar objects found at more distant sites (known as the macrocontext). The pioneer of this form of scientific approach was archaeologist John W. Bennett (1918–). In 1943, he found many copper and shell artifacts in the southeastern United States. Based on where they were found, he decided they must have some religious or ritual significance. Similar finds in Georgia and Oklahoma convinced him that the religious cult that used these objects was widespread.

Context became more important to other scientists as well. Anthropologists study human beings, the way they respond to their physical environment, and the societies in which they live. During the 1940s, anthropologists began to study the way society and culture influence the personalities of individuals. Margaret Mead (1901–1978) wrote *Coming of Age in Samoa* (1928), the classic text using this approach. Her book showed that Samoan girls experienced none of the psychological problems prevalent among American teenagers. This research demonstrated that human psychology was influenced by cultural context, not "preprogrammed" into the brain. During World War II (1939–45), Mead worked for the National Research Council and the Office of War Information (OWI). *Coming of Age in Samoa* was republished for the armed forces by the OWI in 1945. It was used by army planners as they began to reconstruct shattered communities.

Anthropologist Ruth Benedict (1887–1948) was also sponsored by the OWI. After researching Japanese culture and society, she concluded that the wartime behavior of the Japanese could be explained by their culture. The Japanese, she argued, were expected to suppress their emotions and to obey authorities. Benedict's work helped explain behavior that many Americans had considered barbaric. It also influenced U.S. policy toward Japan after 1945. Both anthropologists and archaeologists in the 1940s

The prevailing wind direction across the Pacific is from the west. During World War II (1939–45), the Japanese took advantage of this fact to launch balloon bombs. These were high-altitude balloons carrying bombs intended to fall on the United States. Thousands of balloons were launched, and around three hundred of them came ashore, some as far inland as Iowa and Kansas. Some of the bombs caused wildfires with no casualties, but in Oregon six people were killed. Somehow, the U.S. government managed to keep the balloon-bomb threat secret from the American public, and the Japanese eventually abandoned the idea. Documents from 1944 have since revealed that the Japanese military also was intending to use balloons to spread deadly diseases such as anthrax and plague throughout the United States.

took a more flexible approach to the connection between individuals and their environment. By doing so, they were able to enhance understanding of the past and influence policies for the future.

❖ AIRPLANES GO FASTER THAN SOUND AND ROCKETS BLAST INTO SPACE

During World War II, aircraft were used for many military purposes, from dropping bombs to airlifting supplies and spying on the enemy. Military needs brought great technological improvements, but conventional airplanes with propellers and piston engines had reached their limits by 1945. By then, research had turned toward the jet engine. Other developments in flight technology during the 1940s included the helicopter, the pilotless winged missile, the long-range rocket, and the first true space vehicle.

The demands of war meant that military aviation development had to be carefully organized. Physicist Joseph S. Ames (1864–1943) headed the National Advisory Committee for Aeronautics (NACA). NACA funded research into aerodynamics (the study of the motion of air), engine design, and construction methods and materials. Partly as a result of NACA support, the United States was able to produce 296,000 military aircraft in the 1940s. But NACA's major influence was on airplane design.

By 1945, aircraft were faster, more controllable, and covered greater distances with the same fuel load. By 1949, the Boeing B-39 strategic bomber could carry a four-and-one-half-ton bomb for 9,950 miles. The useful range for heavy bombers had doubled in just three years.

By the early 1940s, designers realized that airplanes driven by propellers could not be improved much further. Though the jet engine had been patented by British inventor Frank Whittle (1907–1996) in 1930, the first jet aircraft did not fly until 1940. The first American jet fighter, the P-59A Airacomet, was not tested until 1942. Early jets lacked power and used a huge amount of fuel. Even so, the German Messerschmitt Me-262 became the first jet aircraft to fly in combat, on July 28, 1944. The first American jet to see military service was the Lockheed F-80 Shooting Star, which was first tested in January 1944. But the F-80 was not used in combat until the Korean War (1950–53).

After 1945, jet propulsion would drive aircraft farther and faster than had ever seemed possible. But until 1947, a barrier lay in the way. As an aircraft flies faster, air pressure builds up on forward-facing surfaces. At around the speed of sound (741 miles per hour at sea level, and slower at higher altitudes), air particles form a barrier (known as the sound barrier) that prevents conventional planes from going any faster.

The X-1 was the first aircraft to fly faster than the speed of sound. Courtesy of the U.S. National Aeronautics and Space Administration.

Aircraft must have special streamlined shapes and extremely powerful engines to penetrate this barrier safely. When they do so, a shock wave creates a loud sound known as a sonic boom. On October 14, 1947, Captain Charles E. "Chuck" Yeager (1923–) flew the rocket-powered X-1 aircraft faster than the speed of sound. He became the first human to break the sound barrier in controlled, level flight. Yeager later flew the plane at its maximum speed of 957 miles per hour.

The X-1's rocket motor produced six thousand pounds of thrust. The rocket was the product of research begun in Germany in the 1920s by scientist Wernher von Braun (1912–1977). Von Braun's V-2 rocket was designed to be used as a long-range missile. It climbed to a height of fifty miles before falling out of control back to earth. More than three thousand of these rockets fell on European cities during the war, most of them on London. After 1945, many V-2s, along with several German rocket scientists, were brought to the United States. American scientists combined the V-2 with their own rocket motor, the Corporal, to create Project Bumper. On February 24, 1949, General Electric and the Jet Propulsion Laboratory (JPL) launched a rocket called Bumper Five. It reached an altitude of 410 kilometers above Earth, becoming the first true space vehicle. Less than fifty years after the first-ever engine-powered airplane flight, the space race had begun.

❖ GENETICS DOMINATES BIOLOGY

Genetics is the branch of biology that explains the way characteristics such as hair and eye color are passed from one generation of a species to the next. In the 1940s, geneticists discovered that the units that specify these characteristics, or genes, are located within chromosomes. Every living thing is made up of billions of small building blocks called cells. Chromosomes are tiny, threadlike structures that exist within each cell. They are made from two types of substances: proteins and nucleic acids. Each chromosome contains a large number of genes, the individual codes that determine an individual's inherited characteristics. Genetics made great strides in the 1940s. But geneticists did not manage to explain how chromosomes were able to carry and transmit information to succeeding generations.

In 1944, at the Rockefeller Institute, a team of scientists made the first step toward solving the puzzle of chromosomes. They discovered that it was nucleic acids, not proteins, in a cell that determined its organism's genetic traits (inherited characteristics). Their research was carried out on a simple organism, the pneumococcal bacterium. But they believed correctly that the same conclusion would be true for humans. A few years later, researcher Barbara McClintock (1902–1992) came up with the idea of "jumping genes." McClintock's theory was that genes could move around on each chromosome between generations. Their influence on one another would change, depending on where they sat relative to each other. Many scientists rejected her idea at first, but it was confirmed in the 1960s. McClintock won the Nobel Prize in 1983 for her work in genetics.

Before the advances in knowledge made during the 1940s, biologists had been split between two different ideas about the way characteristics are inherited. Geneticists looked for genetic information within the organism itself. Evolutionary biologists, who are followers of Charles Darwin (1809–1882), however, saw the environment around the organism as more important than heredity. At a meeting at Princeton, New Jersey in January 1947, the two sides came together for the first time in twenty years. New discoveries in genetics had showed how Darwin's theory of evolution by natural selection could work. Suddenly, geneticists and evolutionary biologists had very little about which to argue. Both groups had turned out to be right.

❖ THE COMPUTER AGE BEGINS

The creation of the first digital computer systems emerged from collaboration among the military, universities, and private businesses. Early computers could weigh as much as thirty tons and were controlled by a series of plugs and wires. But these bulky machines gave the Allied nations a huge advantage in military intelligence during World War II, making it possible for them to decode messages sent by the Germans and the Japanese.

In 1937 International Business Machines (IBM), a manufacturer of typewriters and adding machines, began a joint research project with Harvard University to create a machine that could do calculations automatically. IBM did not expect to make money. Rather, it hoped the success of the project would improve its reputation with the scientific community. The machine that grew out of this collaboration was known as the IBM Automatic Sequence Controlled Calculator, or the Harvard Mark 1 for short. It was demonstrated to Harvard faculty by Howard Aiken (1900–1973) in 1943. The Mark 1 was no more powerful than a 200-era palm-sized scientific calculator. But for the first time, a computer was shown to follow a sequence of commands (a program) and produce accurate final results from raw data. The Mark 1 was used by the U.S. Navy from 1944 onward.

The Mark 1 was an electromechanical machine, relying on electrical currents to move parts of the machine around to create different configurations. It was not unlike a manual telephone exchange and consequently was very slow. But computers soon sped up. In 1944, British mathematician

Early electronic devices used vacuum tubes to amplify electronic signals (make them stronger). They were made of glass and were fragile, heavy, and large. Several tubes were often needed, and they generated a lot of heat and used a lot of electricity. Then in 1947, scientists at the Bell Telephone Laboratories found they could amplify electronic signals by using tiny devices known as transistors. Made from microscopic parts, transistors were tiny, operated at low temperatures, and used around one-twentieth of the power of vacuum tubes. They were also very tough, making them ideal for portable equipment. By the mid-1950s, almost every electronic device contained transistors.

Alan Turing (1912–1954) built a digital computer known as the Colossus. Colossus was used to crack the Enigma code used by the German military to send secret messages. The Enigma code-breaking machine gave Allied military commanders a key advantage when planning the invasion and occupation of mainland Europe. Using the same numbers-based logic system as that employed by Turing, Americans J. Presper Eckert (1919–1995) and John Mauchly (1907–1980) built the ENIAC (Electronic Numerical Integrator and Computer) at the University of Illinois in 1946. The first general-purpose digital computer, ENIAC was about the size of a three-axle truck. In the days before microchips and transistors, the ENIAC contained eighteen thousand fragile glass vacuum tubes and weighed thirty tons.

Computers themselves were in their infancy in the 1940s. But the new field of computer science was already raising many questions about logic, language, and the workings of the human mind. Norbert Wiener (1894–1964) invented the term "cybernetics" to describe his work on the similarities between automatic machines and the human brain. The word itself comes from the Greek word for "steersman." Wiener saw the human nervous system as a system of control and feedback mechanisms, rather like the rudder of a ship. This was exactly the principle used in designing the new computers. Researchers such as Gregory Bateson (1904–1980) and his wife Margaret Mead also asserted that the human brain behaves rather like a machine, in that it has memory, it can associate pieces of data, and it can make choices. Late-twentieth-century research into artificial intelligence has revealed as

The Electronic Numerical Integrator and Computer (ENIAC), the first all-purpose digital computer, was built in 1946. *Courtesy of the Library of Congress.*

many differences as similarities between brains and machines. But Wiener's predictions that cybernetics would provide control mechanisms for artificial limbs and mechanized industry have turned out to be accurate.

❖ SEEING IN THE DARK

The principle of radar, that radio waves bounce back from objects and can be detected by a receiver, was established in 1930 by Lawrence Hyland (1897–1989) at the Naval Research Laboratory. The term "radar" stands for *r*adio *d*etection *a*nd *r*anging. A workable radar device was patented in 1935 by Scottish scientist Robert Watson-Watt (1892–1973). But it was not until 1940 that American radar research became a priority.

In the summer of 1940, Henry Tizard (1885–1959) and a team of scientists arrived in the United States from Britain with the aim of sharing military secrets. The Tizard mission brought with it a machine called the resident cavity magnetron. It was able to produce radiation of much greater intensity than anything American technology could manage at the time. Alfred L. Loomis (1887–1975), head of radar research at the National Defense Research Committee (NDRC), said that the magnetron had advanced American radar research by two years. The NDRC quickly developed the magnetron into an airborne intercept system. By April 1941, the "Rad Lab" at the Massachusetts Institute of Technology (MIT) had built the AI-10, a radar machine capable of detecting airplanes and submarines.

The British were desperate for a radar system to detect attacks from German night bombers. Watson-Watt inspected the AI-10 in 1941, but

American scientists were so confident in the 1940s that they tried to modify the weather. In 1943, Irving Langmuir (1881–1957) and Vincent Schaefer (1906–1993) began to look at ways to make rain. Schaefer eventually came to the conclusion that precipitation (rain, snow, and hail) is created inside supercooled clouds. Such clouds exist below the freezing point, but they also contain both ice crystals and droplets of water. As the ice crystals grow bigger, the water droplets shrink. At a certain point the ice crystals become so big and heavy that they fall to the ground. If they melt on the way down, it rains. If they stay frozen, it snows. Schaefer and Langmuir tried to make precipitation happen artificially. In 1946, Schaefer flew over Mount Greylock in Massachusetts and threw dry ice (a solid form of carbon dioxide) into a cloud. Flying under the cloud, Schaefer noticed a snow flurry. On the ground, his colleague Langmuir was caught in a shower of rain.

found that its radar "shield" was full of holes. He relocated stations and made other adjustments to complete the shield. Soon the Rad Lab had designed the ASV (Air-to-Surface Vessel) radar. The ASV allowed aircraft to detect ships up to five miles away. It was soon installed in B-18 planes to patrol the Atlantic coast. The American system was an even greater success in Britain, where radar stations were positioned along the south and east coasts. German Luftwaffe (airforce) commanders could not understand how the Royal Air Force (RAF) fighter squadrons knew the German bombers were on the way, or how they managed to find them in the dark.

Radar was one of the most important technological developments of World War II. By 1942, the Rad Lab had a budget of $1.15 million per month, and by 1945 it employed around five hundred physicists. The rapid development of radar during the war also was useful after 1945. It made possible the rapid expansion of civilian air transport in the late 1940s and 1950s.

❖ UNLEASHING THE POWER OF THE ATOM

Harnessing the power of the atom is the most significant scientific achievement of the 1940s, and possibly of the entire twentieth century. Nuclear weapons (also known as atomic bombs) brought World War II to

The Atomic Age

Americans became very excited by the possibilities of the atomic age shortly after atomic bombs were dropped on Japan. Within hours, the bartender at the Washington Press Club had invented the Atomic Cocktail, made from pernod and gin. People speculated about potential nuclear-powered cars and aircraft. Some predicted that artificial atomic suns could be created to control the weather. In July 1946, a bomb test on Bikini Atoll in the Pacific Ocean gave its name to the two-piece bathing suit; while in 1947, the Manhattan telephone directory listed forty-five businesses with "atomic" in their names. Popular songs of 1946 and 1947 included "Atom Buster," "Atom Polka," and "Atom Bomb Baby." It was to be a few years before the American public began to appreciate the new dangers of the atomic age.

an abrupt, and some would say early, conclusion. The new technology helped make the United States a dominant force in global affairs and created an entirely new political world order after 1945. Nuclear weaponry created an atmosphere of fear and distrust between nations. But many argue that its deterrent effect helped to prevent a third world war in the twentieth century.

The first controlled atomic chain reaction was achieved in 1942, on an old squash court under the stands of the abandoned Stagg Field football stadium at the University of Chicago. Nobel Prize-winning physicist Enrico Fermi (1901–1954) constructed a nuclear pile (reactor) from six tons of uranium metal and fifty tons of uranium oxide encased in four hundred tons of graphite. On December 2, 1942, the control rods were removed. The pile achieved critical mass when enough of the material had become radioactive to trigger the chain reaction and cause nuclear fission (the splitting of atoms). This was the first-ever controlled release of nuclear energy.

Fermi's work was done in a spirit of scientific inquiry. He and his team simply wanted to see if it could be done. But World War II inspired President Franklin D. Roosevelt to fund research into building the atomic bomb. He was persuaded to do so by German-born Jewish physicist Albert Einstein. Although Einstein was opposed to violence, he feared what would happen if Nazi Germany developed an atomic bomb before the United States did. Less than a month after Fermi's success, the Roosevelt

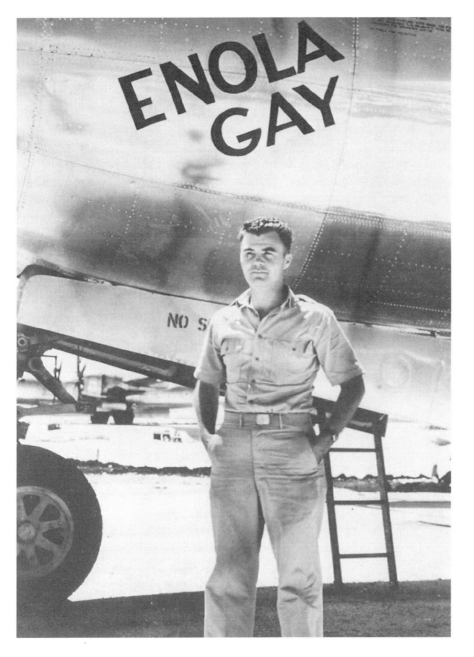

Pilot Paul W. Tibbets
standing beneath the
Enola Gay in 1945. The
Enola Gay was the
military aircraft that
dropped the atomic bomb
on Hiroshima, Japan.
**Reproduced by permission of
the Corbis Corporation.**

administration authorized $400 million for the top-secret Manhattan Project. Headed by General Leslie R. Groves (1896–1970), the Manhattan Project set up research facilities to produce plutonium at Hanford, Washington, and Oak Ridge, Tennessee. In early 1945, the Hanford site began producing pure plutonium, which was perfect for making an atomic bomb.

The Manhattan Project bomb-making research facility was located in New Mexico, at Los Alamos. Under the direction of J. Robert Oppenheimer, scientists at Los Alamos had to solve two problems. First, they had to understand what would happen in the fraction of a second after the chain reaction began, but before the explosion occurred. Understanding this event was essential in order to control the bomb. Second, they had to stop the plutonium from reaching critical mass and exploding too soon. The solution to the second of these problems was to use conventional explosives to encase the plutonium. When these explosives were detonated, the shock wave crushed the plutonium, forcing it to critical mass and triggering the chain reaction that caused the bigger, atomic explosion. Because it was designed to squeeze inward at first, this type of weapon was known as an implosion bomb.

The first atomic bomb was exploded at Alamagordo, in the New Mexico desert, two hundred miles from Los Alamos, on July 16, 1945. The bomb had the power of twenty thousand tons of dynamite. Oppenheimer described the flash as having the "radiance of a thousand suns." Within a month, atomic bombs were made available to the military. On August 6, 1945, the Superfortress bomber *Enola Gay* dropped a uranium bomb called "Little Boy" on the Japanese city of Hiroshima. It destroyed four square miles of the city in a few seconds. Three days later, a plutonium bomb nicknamed "Fat Man" destroyed one-third of the Japanese city of Nagasaki, killing forty thousand people in the blink of an eye. Not long after the bombs were dropped, Einstein was asked how he thought World War III would be fought. He said he did not know, but that World War IV would be fought with sticks and stones.

A September 1945 Gallup poll showed that 65 percent of Americans thought the atomic bomb was "a good thing." Two years later, only 55 percent held that opinion. The dangers of atomic weapons were obvious, and efforts were made to prevent their spread. But the defensive policies of the late 1940s meant that the United States tried to keep nuclear technology to itself. This protectiveness increased the mood of hostility between the Soviet Union and the United States. Efforts to keep the atomic bomb in American hands soon failed. The Soviet Union exploded its own atomic device in 1949.

Because they did not want to be responsible for the destruction of humanity, many scientists opposed further research into atomic weapons. But the government wanted further development. Physicist Edward Teller (1908–) was keen to develop an even more formidable weapon, the hydrogen bomb. The first atomic bombs worked by splitting atoms to release huge amounts of energy in a process known as nuclear fission. Hydrogen

OPPOSITE PAGE
Once released, the atomic bomb causes a gigantic explosion called a "mushroom cloud."
Reproduced by permission of Archive Photos, Inc.

bombs do the opposite; they merge two hydrogen atoms together in a process called nuclear fusion. This is the same chemical reaction that takes place inside the sun. Hydrogen bombs (also known as thermonuclear bombs) are a thousand times more powerful than the bombs that were dropped on Japan. Fearing the Soviet Union's atomic weapons program, President Harry S Truman authorized funding for hydrogen bomb research in 1950.

Nuclear weapons raised many ethical and moral questions. Public opinion was split over the need for atomic bombs, while physicians and biologists warned that radiation from the explosions, also called fallout, was dangerous. Military researchers even went so far as to test the effects of radiation on humans. Soldiers were intentionally exposed to radiation from bomb tests or were given doses of radioactive material by army doctors, who then measured the health effects. Although fear of nuclear accident and war would dominate politics for the next forty years, atomic research in the 1940s did have several positive effects. These included new cancer treatments and the development of nuclear power used to drive ships and generate electricity.

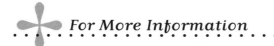 *For More Information*

BOOKS

Allan, Tony. *Understanding DNA: A Breakthrough in Science.* Chicago: Heinemann Library, 2002.

Asimov, Isaac. *How Did We Find Out About Atoms?* New York: Avon Books, 1982.

Bankston, John. *Edward Teller and the Development of the Hydrogen Bomb.* Bear, DE: Mitchell Lane Publishers, 2002.

Brown, Jim. *Radar: How It All Began.* London: Janus, 1996.

Chronicle of the Twentieth Century. Mount Cisco, NY: Chronicle, 1994.

Collier, Christopher, and James Lincoln Collier. *The United States in the Cold War.* New York: Benchmark Books/Marshall Cavendish, 2001.

Cook, Chris, and David Waller, eds. *The Longman Handbook of Modern American History, 1763–1996.* New York: Longman, 1998.

Diggins, John P. *The Proud Decades: America in War and in Peace, 1941–1960.* New York: Norton, 1988.

Editors of Time Life Books. *Decade of Triumph: The 40s.* Alexandria, VA: Time-Life Books, 1999.

Encyclopedia of Technology and Applied Sciences. New York: Marshall Cavendish, 2000.

Hills, Ken. *1940s.* Austin, TX: Raintree Steck-Vaughn, 1992.

Jefferis, David. *Supersonic Flight*. New York: Franklin Watts, 1988.

Kevles, Daniel J. *The Physicists: The History of a Scientific Community in Modern America*. New York: Knopf, 1978.

Keylin, Arleen, and Jonathan Cohen, eds. *The Forties*. New York: Arno Press, 1980.

Larson, Rebecca. *Oppenheimer and the Atomic Bomb*. New York: Franklin Watts, 1988.

Macmillan Encyclopedia of Science. New York: Macmillan Reference, 1997.

McCartney, Scott. *ENIAC: The Triumphs and Tragedies of the World's First Computer*. New York: Walker, 1999.

Nagel, Rob, ed. *U•X•L Encyclopedia of Science*. Detroit: U•X•L, 2001.

Northrup, Mary. *American Computer Pioneers*. Springfield, NJ: Enslow Publishers, 1998.

Rabinowitz, Harold. *Classic Airplanes: Pioneering Aircraft and the Visionaries Who Built Them*. New York: MetroBooks, 1997.

Snedden, Robert. *The History of Genetics*. New York: Thomson Learning, 1995.

Stille, Darlene R. *Extraordinary Women Scientists*. Chicago: Children's Press, 1995.

Stwertka, Albert, and Eve Stwertka. *Physics: From Newton to the Big Bang*. New York: Franklin Watts, 1986.

Taylor, Michael J.H., ed. *Jane's Encyclopedia of Aviation*. New York: Crescent Books, 1993.

Uschan, Michael V. *The 1940s*. San Diego, CA: Lucent Books, 1999.

Wood, Tim, and R.J. Unstead. *The 1940s*. New York: Franklin Watts, 1990.

Yount, Lisa. *Genetics and Genetic Engineering*. New York: Facts on File, 1997.

WEB SITES

American Institute of Physics: Center For History of Physics. [Online] http://www.aip.org/history/ (accessed August 9, 2002).

NASA X-1 Fiftieth Anniversary Homepage. [Online] http://www.hq.nasa.gov/office/pao/History/x1/index.html (accessed August 9, 2002).

chapter eight *Sports*

1940: January 12 The University of Chicago ends its football program, saying that sports are holding back education. Its football stadium later is used for atomic weapons research.

1940: April 3 The Olympic games in Finland are canceled because of the war. The games will not resume until 1948.

1941: Brooklyn Dodgers manager Larry MacPhail orders his team to wear batting helmets.

1941: April 3 Boston University's football team is rocked when all eleven first-string players volunteer for service in the U.S. Naval Corps.

1941: June 2 Baseball hero Lou Gehrig dies of amyotrophic lateral sclerosis (ALS). The disease ended his career and his run of 2,130 consecutive playing appearances. The illness has since become known as "Lou Gehrig's Disease."

1941: July 17 Joe DiMaggio ends his fifty-six-game hitting streak in Cleveland.

1942: January 9 After successfully defending his heavyweight boxing title for the twentieth time, Joe Louis donates his winnings to the Navy Relief Fund.

1942: June 19 In baseball, thirty-nine-year-old Paul Waner of the Boston Braves reaches three thousand career hits in a game against the Pittsburgh Pirates.

1942: December 13 The Washington Redskins win the NFL championship, defeating the Chicago Bears by a score of 14-6.

1943: February 5 Boxer Sugar Ray Robinson is finally defeated by Jake La Motta in ten rounds at Olympia Stadium in Detroit. Robinson had managed to win forty straight bouts up to that point.

1943: June 28 Champion Thoroughbred racehorse Whirlaway retires after winning thirty-two races and $561,161 in prize money.

1944: May 23 The University of Chicago withdraws from all intercollegiate athletic competition.

1944: June 24 The women's Western Golf Open in Chicago is won by Mildred "Babe" Didrikson Zaharias.

1944: November 25 Baseball commissioner Kenesaw Mountain Landis dies at the age of seventy-eight. He is inducted to the Baseball Hall of Fame on December 10.

1944: December 23 In a measure designed to save labor and materials for the war effort, all horse racing is banned effective January 3, 1945.

1945: January 31 Five Brooklyn College basketball players admit to each taking $1,000 bribes to throw (intentionally lose) a game against the University of Akron.

1945: April 24 The position of baseball commissioner, and its $50,000 annual salary, goes to U.S. Senator A. B. "Happy" Chandler.

1945: **May 7** Brooklyn Dodgers co-owner Branch Rickey announces the formation of the six-team Negro Baseball League.

1945: **May 9** The War Mobilization and Reconversion Office lifts the ban on horse racing.

1945: **October 23** Jackie Robinson becomes the first black player to compete in organized professional baseball when he signs with the Brooklyn Dodgers farm team in Montreal (part of the International League).

1946: **January 4** NFL rival league the All-American Football Conference (AAFC) votes to begin its season with an eight-team league.

1946: **March 21** The NFL's twelve-year ban on black players ends when Kenny Washington signs with the Los Angeles Rams.

1946: **December 27** Davis Cup tennis resumes after a six-year suspension due to the war. The U.S. team wins the cup for the first time since 1938.

1947: **April 10** Jackie Robinson becomes the first black player in major league baseball in the twentieth century, after he signs with the Brooklyn Dodgers. In September, he is named rookie of the year by the *Sporting News*.

1947: **September 30** The first televised World Series begins. It is sponsored by Gillette Safety Razor and Ford Motor Company, each of whom pay $65,000 for the privilege.

1947: **December 5** Despite being knocked down twice, Joe Louis successfully defends his heavyweight title against "Jersey" Joe Walcott.

1948: **January 30** The fifth Winter Olympiad, and the first Olympic games held since 1936, opens in St. Moritz, Switzerland.

1948: **June 25** In a rematch with Joe Walcott Joe Louis retains his heavyweight title for the twenty-fifth and last time. After knocking out Walcott in the eleventh round, Louis announces his retirement the following day.

1949: **March 7** American League batting champion Ted Williams becomes the highest-paid baseball player ever when he signs with the Boston Red Sox for $100,000 per year.

1949: **August 3** The National Basketball Association (NBA) is formed when the Basketball Association of America and the National Basketball League merge.

1949: **November 19** Jackie Robinson becomes the first black player to be named the National League's Most Valuable Player by the Baseball Writers' Association.

Overview

In the early 1940s, sports organizations tried to entertain Americans. But after the Japanese attack on Pearl Harbor on December 7, 1941, disruption in sports schedules could not be avoided. Most professional and college athletes were eligible for military service, and those who were qualified soon signed up. Millions of American women went to work in factories during World War II, and women athletes found themselves in demand as the shortage of male sports talent grew worse. In 1943 the entire major league baseball season was on the brink of cancellation. Philip Wrigley, owner of the Chicago Cubs, and Branch Rickey, owner of the Brooklyn Dodgers, invented the All-American Girls Baseball League (AAGBL). The new league did not last long, but it was very popular in the absence of male baseball stars. Elsewhere, women athletes made more permanent gains. In golf, for example, Mildred "Babe" Didrikson Zaharias and Patty Berg became major stars.

After the war, professional sports began to turn into big business. The hardships of the Great Depression (1930–39) were over, and attendance at sports events began to rise. Television brought increased audiences to games and extra money for advertisers. Sports also became better organized. In the early 1940s, for example, professional basketball was without a players' union. Athletes earned $50 per week and played 150 games in a season. In 1949, the National Basketball Association (NBA) was set up to organize basketball on a national level. In baseball, players negotiated a minimum salary of $5,500 per year in 1947 and persuaded the owners to set up a pension fund for retired and injured ball players.

As travel became easier with the new aircraft technology and as television spread across the country, salaries for top players shot up. By 1950,

St. Louis Cardinals baseball player Stan Musial was earning almost ten times the minimum salary. In football, too, wages rose sharply. From $150 per game in 1940, football players earned an average salary of $5,000 per season in 1949. Top athletes in individual sports did even better. Champion heavyweight boxer Joe Louis commanded well over $100,000 per fight. On the Professional Golfers' Association (PGA) tour, winners took home $12,000 in prize money for each tournament. In 1947, tennis star Jack Kramer signed a deal that gave him $50,000 against ticket sales for his international tour.

As sports became richer and the number of fans began to grow, racial barriers started to break down. When African American Jackie Robinson joined the Brooklyn Dodgers in April 1947, he broke the color barrier in professional baseball. Within a few years, a handful of black players had become among the best in the game. In the South, blacks and whites did not play sports together, even in colleges, until late in the decade. But in most sports in the 1940s, black athletes took a greater role in what were once all-white teams.

After 1945, American sports gradually became part of the entertainment industry. New professional organizations and commissions modified the rules of play to ensure maximum entertainment value. Players became national heroes and were used by advertisers to sell goods of all kinds. Many sportswriters complained that sports and athletes had been corrupted by greed. But television and advertising money paid for better training grounds and improved facilities for fans. Between 1946 and 1952, the income major league baseball received from television rose from one million to five million dollars. Athletes delighted fans with more and more spectacular achievements. After the hardships of depression and war, American sports helped create a new, optimistic national mood.

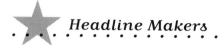

Eddie Arcaro (1916–1997) Fourteen-year-old Eddie Arcaro quit school to ride racehorses. He went on to become one of horse racing's most successful jockeys, winning the Triple Crown twice, and winning over four thousand victories by 1958. In 1941, he rode Whirlaway to victory in the Kentucky Derby and went on to win the Triple Crown. In 1946, he collected more than $1 million in winnings, the most money ever won by a single jockey in a year. Yet Arcaro always praised his horses. "You seldom hear of a jockey getting into a slump riding good horses," he said. *Photo reproduced by permission of AP/Wide World Photos.*

Patricia "Patty" Berg (1918–) A childhood athlete, Patricia "Patty" Berg was one of the leading woman golfers from the 1940s to the 1960s. She began playing tournaments while a student at the University of Minnesota in the late 1930s. She won forty amateur titles before signing a sponsorship deal with Wilson Sporting Goods Company of Chicago in 1940. In the 1940s, she won the Women's Western Open title three times, and the first U.S. Women's National Open in 1946. By 1981, when she stopped competing, she had eighty-three pro tournament victories to her name. *Photo reproduced by permission of AP/Wide World Photos.*

Felix "Doc" Blanchard (1924–) Between 1944 and 1946, Felix "Doc" Blanchard and his fellow running back Glenn Davis (1925–) led the Army football team to twenty-seven victories, including national titles in 1944 and 1945. Together, Blanchard and Davis brought brute strength and blinding speed to the team's backfield. In 1945, Blanchard became the first junior to win the Heisman Trophy, which is annually awarded to the nation's best football player. He was the first football player to win the James Sullivan Award as the best amateur athlete, and the first person to win both awards. He remained in the Army Air Corps as a pilot for the next twenty-five years. *Photo reproduced by permission of the Corbis Corporation.*

Joe DiMaggio (1914–1999) Joe DiMaggio is one of the most revered figures in American sport. Playing for the New York Yankees, he won three Most Valuable Player awards, while his 1941 hitting streak of fifty-six games fascinated the nation. With a career batting average of .325 and a total of 361 home runs, DiMaggio was a superb athlete. The son of Italian immigrants, six-foot-two-inch "Joltin' Joe" was the American League's first $100,000-a-year player. He retired in 1952, turning down another $100,000 contract, saying: "When baseball is no longer fun, it's no longer a game." DiMaggio entered baseball's Hall of Fame in 1955. *Photo reproduced by permission of the Corbis Corporation.*

Joe Louis (1914–1981) On June 22, 1937, Joe Louis knocked out heavyweight James J. Braddock (1905–1974) to become the youngest heavyweight boxing champion in history. Louis was the first black champ in more than twenty years. He successfully defended his title a record twenty-five consecutive times, retiring unbeaten in 1938. During that time, radio broadcasts of his contests attracted fifty million listeners. When he died, Louis lay in state at Caesar's Palace Sports Pavilion in Las Vegas, Nevada. His body was flown aboard Air Force One to Washington, D.C., where he was buried at Arlington National Cemetery. *Photo reproduced by permission of the Corbis Corporation.*

Larry MacPhail (1890–1975) As a baseball team owner, Larry MacPhail thought he should attract paying fans and put on a show for them. Between 1934 and 1937, he made a financial and sporting success of the struggling Cincinnati Reds. After buying the Brooklyn Dodgers in 1938, he promoted every game as a grudge match to attract fans. After the war, he moved on to the New York Yankees. After the Yankees won the World Series in 1947, MacPhail punched a sportswriter and promptly sold his interest in the team. He attributed his long life to leaving baseball before the excitement killed him. *Photo reproduced by permission of AP/Wide World Photos.*

Jackie Robinson (1919–1972) A remarkable all-around athlete, Jackie Robinson is famous for being the first black player in major league baseball. Brooklyn Dodgers manager Branch Rickey (1881–1965) deliberately hired him to end segregation in baseball. Robinson was told that Rickey wanted a black player who had the guts not to respond to racist taunts. At times, Robinson and his wife feared for their lives. In 1949, his third season with the Dodgers, he won the league's Most Valuable Player award. Robinson was elected to the Baseball Hall of Fame in 1962, the first year he was eligible. *Photo reproduced by permission of Archive Photos, Inc.*

Mildred "Babe" Didrikson Zaharias (1911–1956) Mildred "Babe" Didrikson Zaharias is generally thought to be the greatest female athlete who ever lived. One sportswriter said that short of winning the Kentucky Derby, there was nothing she couldn't do. She could hit home runs and score baskets, and she was a record-breaking javelin thrower and hurdler. She was amateur and professional champion in many sports, including golf, and was named American Woman Athlete of the year in 1932. She died of cancer at the age of fifty-four. *Photo reproduced by permission of the Corbis Corporation.*

◆◆◆ *Topics in the News* •

❖ AUTOMOBILE RACING REVIVES AFTER THE WAR

Two types of auto racing dominated the 1940s. Indy racing featured specially built race cars and took place on paved speedways and racetracks. The most famous of these races was the Indianapolis 500. Stock car racing, by contrast, was quite different. Usually run on dirt tracks of compacted clay, stock car races featured modified road cars that often had been rescued from junkyards. Many of the stock car drivers of the 1940s had learned their skills while smuggling illegal liquor, a job in which a talent for high-speed driving was essential for escaping the police.

In 1940 and 1941, Wilbur Shaw (1902–1954) was the star driver of the Indianapolis series. With his third victory in 1940, he became the first driver to win two Indianapolis 500 races in a row. But in 1941, while leading the race in the closing stages, Shaw's car lost a tire and spun into a concrete barrier, ending his driving career. The race was won by future star Mauri Rose (1906–1981). The Indianapolis speedway lay idle from 1942 to 1945, when it was bought by Tony Hulman (1901–1977). Along with his manager, the ex-driver Shaw, Hulman is credited with saving the Indianapolis Motor Speedway after World War II.

The second half of the decade belonged to Rose, Bill Holland (1907–1984), and their Blue Crown Special team. In 1947, Holland was leading Rose with eight laps to go. The two drivers were told to hold their positions, but Holland, thinking he was a lap ahead, waved Rose through to win the race. Rose and Holland split the winnings of $137,425. The Rose-Holland duel was repeated in the next two years, with Rose winning again in 1948, and Holland setting a new track record of four hours and ten minutes to take his only Indianapolis 500 victory in 1949. By then, the Indy 500 was America's top auto race.

The other main form of auto racing in the 1940s was stock car racing. In 1946, a competitive Indianapolis 500 race car cost around $30,000. A stock car, by contrast, could go from junkyard to racetrack for $2,500. They were called stock cars because they looked like normal road cars. Bill France (1909–1992) made stock car racing more respectable when he founded the National Association for Stock Car Racing (NASCAR) in 1948. The inaugural race was held at the Charlotte (North Carolina) Speedway on June 19, 1949. Moving away from the traditional stock car image, the idea was to race late-model cars less than three years old. Fans enjoyed watching cars similar to those they saw on the street battling it out on the track. Soon companies such as Ford realized that NASCAR was

Indianapolis 500 Winners

Year	Driver(s)	Car	Average Speed (mph)
1940	Wilbur Shaw	Maserati	114.277
1941	F. Davis and M. Rose	Wetteroth-Offy	115.117
1946	George Robson	Adams-Sparks	114.820
1947	Mauri Rose	Deidt-Offy	116.338
1948	Mauri Rose	Deidt-Offy	119.814
1949	Bill Holland	Deidt-Offy	121.327

The race was not run between 1942 and 1945 because of World War II.

an important marketing opportunity, and they supplied cars for the races. As with other sports in the 1940s, auto racing was becoming part of both the entertainment industry and the advertising industry.

❖ BASEBALL GOES TO WAR

America's favorite sport began the 1940s with outstanding performances from future Hall-of-Famers Bob Feller (1918–), Joe DiMaggio (1914–1999), and Ted Williams (1918–2002). Feller won twenty-seven games for the Cleveland Indians in 1940. In their final game of the season, the Indians lost to the Detroit Tigers, who went on to lose the World Series to the Cincinnati Reds. It was the Reds' first world championship in over two decades. The 1941 season was even more spectacular. Williams, of the Boston Red Sox, became the first player in history to crack the .400 batting average barrier for the season, finishing with a batting average of .406. But his achievement was overshadowed by DiMaggio's record-breaking hitting streak. Between May 15 and July 17, DiMaggio reached base safely for a record fifty-six consecutive games, breaking a mark set back in 1897. He won the American League's Most Valuable Player award, and his team, the New York Yankees, went on to win the World Series. It was the first of four World Series wins for the Yankees in the 1940s.

After the Japanese attack on Pearl Harbor on December 7, 1941, large numbers of ball players volunteered for, or were drafted into, military service. By 1942, 328 out of 607 major leaguers had signed up. Baseball commissioner Kenesaw Mountain Landis (1866–1944) considered closing down the major leagues for the duration of the war. But President Franklin D. Roosevelt (1882–1945) urged him to keep the game going as long as no players tried to avoid the draft. The shortage of younger talent during the

war meant that older and less-capable players enjoyed fleeting fame. For example, Pete Gray (1917–) signed with the St. Louis Browns in 1945 at age twenty-eight and played seventy-seven games, finishing the season with a mediocre batting average of .218. What made Gray unusual was that he had only one arm. When he caught the ball in the outfield he would throw it in the air, throw the glove off his left and only hand, catch the ball, and throw it back into play.

After 1945, baseball was shaken up again when African American Jackie Robinson (1919–1972) was signed by the Brooklyn Dodgers. Robinson was an extraordinary athlete, and Dodgers manager Branch Rickey (1881–1965) was keen to have him in the lineup. But he knew Robinson would face tough times as the only black player in the major leagues. On April 15, 1947, Robinson played first base for the Dodgers in a game against the Boston Braves at Ebbets Field. Robinson did all that his manager asked of him and more. Many white players threatened to strike if they had to play against Robinson, but the fans did not support them. Robinson kept his cool when taunted with racist comments and was voted Rookie of the Year, finishing the season with a batting average of .297. In 1949, he won Most Valuable Player honors, closing with a .342 average. Robinson finished his career batting .311 over ten seasons.

Stars like DiMaggio, Feller, Williams, and Stan Musial (1920–) returned from military service to resume their careers in the late 1940s. DiMaggio beat Ted Williams (1918–) to the Most Valuable Player award in 1947. In 1948 the Cleveland Indians, with star pitchers Feller and Satchel Paige (c.1907–1982), won their first American League pennant since 1920; the Boston Braves took the National League title for the first time since 1914. The Indians went on to win the World Series. In 1948, the New York Yankees went up against traditional rivals the Brooklyn Dodgers in the World Series. The Yankees won in a year when twenty million Americans paid to attend major and minor league baseball games. Since 1947, many fans had also watched the games on television. At the end of the 1940s, baseball was booming.

❖ BASKETBALL PLAYS BY NEW RULES

At the start of the 1940s, basketball was still adapting to a 1938 rule change that ended the need for a jump ball after every basket. The game had speeded up as a result, and a new shot, the jump shot, had become the major offensive weapon for most teams. Basketball was generally less affected by World War II than other sports. But the draft did have one strange effect. Many basketball players were rejected by the military because they were too tall! Because of this, the average height of teams

OPPOSITE PAGE
Baseball players like Joe DiMaggio left the game to fight in World War II.
Reproduced by permission of AP/Wide World Photos.

Women's Baseball

In 1943, half of all major league baseball players were overseas serving in the armed forces. The game was in crisis. President Franklin D. Roosevelt (1882–1945) urged baseball franchise owners to keep the game going. Chicago Cubs owner and chewing gum millionaire Philip K. Wrigley (1894–1977), and Brooklyn Dodgers general manager Branch Rickey (1881–1965) came up with the idea of the All-American Girls Baseball League (AAGBL). Taking players from amateur softball leagues, they set up a four-team league and offered the players excellent pay. The players' background in softball meant they did not pitch overhand until 1948. The league's first star was Dorothy "Dottie" Kamenshek (1926–). Kamenshek could hit the ball all over the field. She struck out only 81 times out of 3,736 at-bats. The AAGBL was very popular, but as male baseball stars returned from the war after 1945, it began to fade. The AAGBL folded in 1954. It was remembered in the 1992 movie *A League of Their Own*.

crept up as the war went on. By 1945, Oklahoma A&M coach Hank Iba (1904–1993) could announce the "tallest team on earth." Built around seven-footer Bob "Foothills" Kurland (1925–), Iba's team was so tall that it forced new goaltending rules.

The Kentucky Wildcats dominated the postwar collegiate game. They took the National Conference of Collegiate Athletics (NCAA) title four times between 1945 and 1954. In 1949, Kentucky established twenty-two NCAA individual and team records. After the war, black athletes attending college after military service also transformed college basketball. In 1946, for example, Charles "Chuck" Cooper (1926–1984) began playing for Duquesne University. Many southern teams refused to play Duquesne when Cooper was in the lineup. The National Basketball Association (NBA) was formed in 1949 when the Basketball Association of America (BAA) and the National Basketball League (NBL) merged under the leadership of Maurice Podoloff (1890–1985). Cooper later became the first black player in the NBA.

Although mixed-race teams were unknown in the professional game during the 1940s, the all-black Harlem Globetrotters were one of the few professional teams to be financially secure. They won the world professional championship in 1940. The Globetrotters were so skillful that coach Abe Saperstein (1903–1966) instructed them to play hard for the

Pitcher Jean Marlowe played for the Chicago Colleens of the All American Girls Baseball League. While male baseball stars were at war, the league enjoyed success but folded in 1954, when major league baseball players returned. *Reproduced by* **permission of the Corbis Corporation.**

first ten minutes, build a lead, and then relax and put on a show. They soon became international stars, touring the world and even performing for Pope Pius XII (1876–1958). The Globetrotters often distracted their opponents by making them laugh, but their skills were as impressive as

their humor. Many of their trick shots, such as the no-look pass, became standard plays in basketball.

Rule changes in the 1940s turned basketball into a high-speed, exciting game. Stars such as the Philadelphia Warriors' Joe Fulks (1921–1976) averaged over twenty points per game, a high scoring average at the time. Fulks actually managed to score over thirty points on twelve occasions, and he scored forty-one in one memorable game. Six-foot-ten-inch George Mikan (1924–) also boosted the game's appeal. Playing for the Minneapolis Lakers for six years, Mikan led the league in scoring three times. His career scoring average on his retirement in 1954 was 22.4 points per game. Before he retired, Mikan forced yet another rule change. His incredible control inside the paint led the NBA to widen the lanes underneath the basket to twelve feet.

❖ PROMOTERS TAKE OVER BOXING

One fighter dominated American boxing in the 1940s: Joe Louis (1914–1981), heavyweight champion from 1937 until 1949. Tens of thousands of fans came to see his fights, even when he faced weak opposition. Surveys showed that around fifty million radio listeners in the early 1940s tuned in to Joe Louis's fights. For a period in 1940 and 1941, Louis took on a challenger every month. Louis was sometimes criticized for fighting members of the so-called "bum-of-the-month club." Boxing promoters grew rich and powerful on his success, but they also had serious problems to worry about: keeping out the gangsters and the gamblers.

Organized crime had always been interested in boxing. As the sport became more popular, and the amount of prize money involved grew larger, crime syndicates, such as a group known as Murder Incorporated, took more of an interest. In the late 1940s, the mob's "commissioner" of boxing was Frankie "Jimmy the Wop" Carbo (1904–1976), a professional killer first arrested for murder at the age of twenty. Carbo bragged under oath that he controlled boxing. In the middleweight division, corruption was widespread. Boxers Jake La Motta (1921–), Rocky Graziano (1922–1990), one-time champion Tony Zale (1913–1997), and many others were involved in staged fights in which the outcome was predetermined. The mob made a great deal of money from illegal gambling, and many fighters were paid to lose fights intentionally in the 1940s.

Sugar Ray Robinson (1921–1989) was so dominant in the welterweight division that he seemed to be above suspicion. When he turned professional in 1940, at the age of twenty, he had won all eighty-five of his amateur fights, sixty-nine by knockout. But in 1947, Robinson changed his story over a reported bribe, and the boxing commission punished him for sus-

OPPOSITE PAGE
The Harlem Globetrotters was the first successful all-black professional basketball team.
Reproduced by permission of the Corbis Corporation.

The Bronx Bull

The most famous case of corruption in boxing was that of "The Bronx Bull" Jake La Motta (1921–). In June 1947 La Motta was offered $100,000 to lose a contest with Tony Janiro (1927–). He said he would do so if his next bout could be a championship fight, but the bosses refused. La Motta, weighing 155 pounds, battered Janiro for ten rounds. After being investigated and fined for cheating in another fight, La Motta was offered his chance at the title against France's Marcel Cerdan (1916–1949). To organize the bout, La Motta had to pay mobster Frankie Carbo (1904–1976) $20,000. La Motta's purse for the fight was just $19,000, but he bet $10,000 on himself to win, and he did. The rematch looked set to be La Motta's big payday, but his opponent Cerdan was killed in a plane crash on his way to the United States.

pected cheating. Heavyweight Joe Louis was never seriously suspected of cheating, however. His reputation with the public rose even higher when he became Private Joe Louis of the U.S. Army on January 10, 1942. In 1946, Louis fought a rematch with Billy Conn (1917–1993), a fighter he had beaten in 1941. At $100 each, the cost of ringside seats hit a record high. Over forty-five thousand people watched Louis knock out Conn in the eighth round of a disappointing fight. Though Louis earned a record $625,916, it was not quite enough to cover his debts, back taxes, and the cost of his entourage: twenty-three minders, trainers, and managers.

By the end of the decade, boxing was a big-money sport. Live audiences alone raised $1.25 million a year for Madison Square Garden, while radio and television brought in millions more. In 1949, the Tournament of Champions promoters merged with Joe Louis Promotions to become the International Boxing Club (IBC). Louis himself retained a 20-percent share of the IBC and a salary of $20,000. By 1950 the IBC controlled half of all championship fights in America. The age of the mass media and corporate control of boxing had arrived.

❖ FOOTBALL ENTERS THE MODERN ERA

College football was transformed in the 1940s by one important rule change. The free-substitution rule allowed a coach to make any number of substitutions at any time during a game except in the last two minutes of the first half. Before the 1941 season, eleven players on each team had played the entire game, and could be substituted for only if they were injured. With many college players serving in the military, the new rule meant that war-weakened teams could still compete at the highest level. University of Michigan football coach Fritz Crisler (1899–1982) introduced the platoon system on October 13, 1945 in a game against Army. In Crisler's system, players specialized in a particular part of the game, such as short-yardage offense, passing offense, and the corresponding defensive plays. Before long, teams' rosters had swelled to as many as 120 men.

World War II dealt a major blow to both college and professional football. With so many players in the military, around 350 college teams closed down during the war, including the University of Chicago. The one team to benefit was Army. College players often went to West Point and played for the Army team. In 1944, Army averaged fifty-six points per game, a modern record. In the National Football League (NFL), the 1941 season belonged to the Chicago Bears. But their championship game against the New York Giants came just two weeks after Pearl Harbor and was attended by only 13,341 fans.

With 638 of its players serving in the military, the NFL used older players, draft-deferred players, and merged teams. In 1943, the league still averaged a respectable 23,644 spectators at each game, a jump of 39 percent compared to 1942. By 1944, the NFL had been reduced to eight teams. The NFL made stars of its best players, and one of the greatest during the war era was Bill Dudley (1921–). He was the last great two-way (offensive and defensive) player, and the only player voted as most valuable at the college, the armed services, and professional levels. When he returned from the war in 1945, he signed with the Detroit Lions for a record-breaking $20,000.

After 1945, college and professional football leagues enjoyed a revival. With athletes back on campus, college teams such as Notre Dame wanted to avenge recent defeats at the hands of Army. When those two teams met at the end of 1946, there were fourteen future all-American players and ten future Hall-of-Famers on the field, yet the final score was 0-0. Late in the decade, the professional All-American Football Conference (AAFC) was set up by *Chicago Tribune* sports editor Arch Ward (1896–1955). Player salaries rocketed from $150 a game in 1941 to an average of $5,000 for a ten-game season in 1949. The stars earned much more. In 1946, the NFL Rams moved from Cleveland to Los Angeles, and the AAFC moved teams into San Francisco and Los Angeles, making football the first major-league sport on the West Coast. But the competition for fans was too intense. By 1947 the U.S. economy would not support two high-paying leagues, and the two merged.

An American Boy Wonder

The 1940 and 1944 Olympics were canceled because of World War II. At the 1948 Summer Olympics in London, the United States won eleven events, Sweden won five, and eight other countries won one each. American boy wonder Bob Mathias (1930–) was the outstanding athlete of the 1948 summer games. Having competed in his first decathlon only six weeks earlier, he won gold in this most grueling of Olympic challenges. But in case anyone wondered if his win was a fluke, he went on to be the American decathlon champion in 1949 and 1950. He repeated his Olympic success in 1952 at Helsinki, Finland. Interviewed after taking the gold medal in 1948, the seventeen-year-old Mathias was asked what he would do next. He replied: "Start shaving, I guess."

❖ GOLF CLUBS ADVISED TO PLOW THE ROUGH

Around a quarter of the golf courses in the United States were closed during World War II. Members of the courses that stayed open worked hard, not only to help the war effort but also to make sure the game did not put pressure on war industries or the military. At most courses, members began carrying their own clubs when their caddies went off to fight. Other members mowed the greens and fairways themselves and refurbished old golf clubs in a recycling craze. Millions of golf balls were dredged up from the bottom of lakes to be reused. Members of the Black Rock Club in Atlanta were embarrassed when sixteen thousand lost balls were recovered from their lake. The United States Golf Association (USGA) suggested that the roughs should be plowed and planted with vegetables to boost wartime food supplies. Few clubs acted on that idea, but the Augusta National Golf Course was turned over to grazing cattle in 1943 while the Masters tournament was suspended.

Between 1942 and 1945, all major USGA events were canceled, including the U.S. Open, the U.S. Amateur, and the Women's Amateur. The U.S. Open was replaced with the Hale American Open. Played in Chicago, the Hale raised $20,000 for the war effort. By 1943, there were 350 Professional Golfers' Association (PGA) members serving in the military. Among them were stars such as Sam Snead (1912–2002), Lawson Little (1910–1968), and Jimmy Demaret (1910–1983). Their Christmas gift from the Professional Golfers' Association (PGA) was a carton of cigarettes.

Golfer Byron Nelson dominated professional golf during the 1940s.
Reproduced by permission of AP/Wide WWorld Photos.

The golfer who dominated the game during the war years was Byron Nelson (1912–). Because competition was in short supply during the war years, it is difficult to measure Nelson's greatness in terms of the golfers he actually beat. But his consistency cannot be disputed. He won eight tournaments in 1944 and eighteen in 1945, for a total of twenty-six wins out of fifty-one starts. He collected $66,000 in war bond prizes in 1945, and finished in the money in 112 consecutive tournaments. For 120 tournament rounds, his average score for eighteen holes was 68.33. Assuming the course average par was 71, Nelson was 320-under-par for all his rounds of tournament play in 1945. It was one of the most remarkable winning streaks in golfing history.

Though the men's game was on its way to becoming a major sport in the 1940s, women's golf was hardly even organized. In 1946, the Women's Professional Golfers' Association (WPA) was formed; just three years later, a rival organization appeared: the Ladies' Professional Golfers' Association (LPGA). Funded by money from Weathervane clothing products, the LPGA helped promote Weathervane through a four-course tournament with a purse of $15,000. The tournament was dominated by Mildred "Babe" Didrikson Zaharias (1911–1956) and Patty Berg (1918–). They helped make women's golf a popular spectator sport in the 1950s.

❖ TENNIS PLAYERS TURN PRO

By the 1940s, a small group of professional tennis players was touring the world and playing for small audiences. The Professional Lawn Tennis Association (PLTA) had been around for nearly twenty years. But the United States Lawn Tennis Association (USLTA), an amateur association, did not take the PLTA very seriously. Despite the fact that popular players, such as Great Britain's Fred Perry (1909–1995) and America's Ellsworth Vines (1911–1944), were playing as professionals in the late 1930s, professional tennis was not as popular as the amateur game. To make matters worse, professional tours and tournaments were suspended after 1942 because of the war.

Jack Kramer (1921–) was the first player to make professional tennis popular with fans. In 1946 and 1947, he won the United States Outdoor Championship, and he took the Wimbledon singles and doubles titles in 1947. A flashy player of what became known as "attack tennis," Kramer was loved by the fans. The secret of his success was an all-out offensive style. He won the first four tournaments of 1947 without losing a set and without having his serve broken. When he turned professional in 1948, going on an eighty-nine-game tour with former Wimbledon champion Bobby Riggs (1918–1995), professional tennis began a postwar revival. Traveling five thousand miles a month, the touring players earned gross revenues of $383,000. Kramer was pro champion in 1948; he lost to Riggs in 1949.

Amateur tennis also had its attractions after World War II. Gertrude Augusta Moran (1923–), better known as Gorgeous Gussie, was knocked out of the Wimbledon tournament in the third round in 1949. But although Moran had been expected to do well, it was not her poor performance that caused a stir. Moran had wanted to play in a colored dress, but court officials persuaded her not to; instead, she upset the All-England Club with a display of lace panties never before seen on court. Gorgeous Gussie and her "undignified" attire made front-page news in London. The All-England Club imposed a very strict dress code at Wimbledon from then on. In 1950, Moran took her glamorous image and her frilly knickers on the professional tennis tour with Riggs, Kramer, and other male tennis stars.

For More Information

BOOKS

Aaseng, Nathan. *Women Olympic Champions.* San Diego, CA: Lucent Books, 2001.

Anderson, Dave. *The Story of Basketball.* New York: W. Morrow, 1997.

Bacho, Peter. *Boxing in Black and White.* New York: Henry Holt, 1999.

Bak, Richard. *Joe Louis: The Great Black Hope.* New York: Da Capo Press, 1998.

Bayne, Bijan C. *Sky Kings: Black Pioneers of Professional Basketball.* New York: Franklin Watts, 1997.

Camper, Erich. *Encyclopedia of the Olympic Games.* New York: McGraw Hill, 1972.

Christopher, Matt. *Great Moments in Baseball History.* Boston: Little, Brown, 1996.

Collins, Ace, and John Hillman. *Blackball Superstars: Legendary Players of the Negro Baseball Leagues.* Greensboro, NC: Avisson Press, 1999.

Cooper, Michael L. *Playing America's Game: The Story of Negro League Baseball.* New York: Lodestar Books, 1993.

Dunnahoo, Terry Janson, and Herma Silverstein. *Baseball Hall of Fame.* New York: Maxwell Macmillan International, 1994.

Greenspan, Bud. *100 Greatest Moments in Olympic History.* Los Angeles: General Publishing Group, 1995.

Grimsley, Will. *Tennis: Its History, People, and Events.* Englewood Cliffs, NJ: Prentice Hall. 1971.

Gross, John, and the editors of *Golf Magazine. The Encyclopedia of Golf.* New York: Harper and Row, 1979.

Hollander, Zander. *Home Run: Baseball's Greatest Hits and Hitters.* New York: Random House, 1984.

Italia, Bob. *100 Unforgettable Moments in Pro Tennis.* Edina, MN: Abdo & Daughters, 1996.

Kahn, Roger. *Games We Used to Play.* New York: Tickner and Fields, 1992.

Liss, Howard. *They Changed the Game: Football's Great Coaches, Players, and Games.* Philadelphia: Lippincott, 1975.

Peper, George. *The Story of Golf.* New York: TV Books, 1999.

Robinson, Max, and Jack Kramer, editors. *The Encyclopedia of Tennis: One Hundred Years of Great Players and Events.* New York: Viking, 1974.

Ryan, Pat. *The Heavyweight Championship.* Mankato, MN: Creative Education, 1993.

Smith, Robert. *Illustrated History of Pro Football.* New York: Madison Square, 1970.

Stewart, Mark. *Baseball: A History of the National Pastime.* New York: Franklin Watts, 1998.

Stewart, Mark. *Basketball: A History of Hoops.* New York: Franklin Watts, 1998.

Uschan, Michael V. *Golf.* San Diego, CA: Lucent Books, 2001.

Wallenchinsky, David. *The Complete Book of the Olympics.* New York: Viking, 1984.

Whittingham, Richard. *Rites of Autumn: The Story of College Football.* New York: Free Press, 2001.

Wind, Herbert Warren. *The Story of American Golf.* New York: Callaway Editions, 2000.

WEB SITES

College Football Hall of Fame. [Online] http://www.collegefootball.org/ (accessed February 2002).

Cyber Boxing Zone. [Online] http://cyberboxingzone.com/ (accessed April 2002).

Major League Baseball History. [Online] http://mlb.mlb.com/NASApp/mlb/mlb/history/mlb_history_awards.jsp (accessed April 2002).

National Baseball Hall Of Fame. [Online] http://www.baseballhalloffame.org/ (accessed April 2002).

Pro Football Hall of Fame. [Online] http://www.profootballhof.com/ (accessed April 2002).

Women in Baseball: All-American Girls' Professional Baseball League. [Online] http://www.acusd.edu/%7Ejsartan/AAGBL.htm (accessed April 2002).

Where to Learn More

BOOKS

Aaseng, Nathan. *Women Olympic Champions*. San Diego, CA: Lucent Books, 2001.

Allan, Tony. *Understanding DNA: A Breakthrough in Science*. Chicago: Heinemann Library, 2002.

Ambrose, Stephen E. *Citizen Soldiers: The U.S. Army from the Normandy Beaches to the Bulge to the Surrender of Germany, June 7, 1944–May 7, 1945*. New York: Simon & Schuster, 1998.

Anderson, Dale. *The Cold War Years*. Austin, TX: Raintree/Steck-Vaughn, 2001.

Anderson, Dave. *The Story of Basketball*. New York: William Morrow, 1997.

Asimov, Isaac. *How Did We Find Out About Atoms?* New York: Avon Books, 1982.

Awmiller, Craig. *This House on Fire: The Story of the Blues*. New York: Franklin Watts, 1996.

Bacho, Peter. *Boxing in Black and White*. New York: Henry Holt, 1999.

Bailey, Donna. *Dancing*. Austin, TX: Raintree/Steck-Vaughn, 1991.

Bak, Richard. *Joe Louis: The Great Black Hope*. New York: Da Capo Press, 1998.

Baker, Patricia. *Fashions of a Decade: The 1940s*. New York: Facts on File, 1992.

Balliett, Whitney. *American Musicians: Fifty Portraits in Jazz*. New York: Oxford University Press, 1986.

Bankston, John. *Edward Teller and the Development of the Hydrogen Bomb*. Bear, DE: Mitchell Lane Publishers, 2002.

Barnes, Rachel. *Abstract Expressionists*. Chicago, IL: Heinemann Library, 2002.

Bayne, Bijan C. *Sky Kings: Black Pioneers of Professional Basketball*. New York: Franklin Watts, 1997.

Bender, Lionel. *Frontiers of Medicine*. New York: Gloucester Press, 1991.

Benton, Mike. *The Comic Book in America: An Illustrated History*. Dallas, TX: Taylor, 1989.

Bernard, Sheila Curran, and Sarah Mondale, eds. *School: The Story of American Public Education*. Boston: Beacon Press, 2001.

Bordley, James, and A. McGehee Harvey. *Two Centuries of American Medicine, 1776–1976*. Philadelphia: Saunders, 1976.

Bredeson, Carmen. *American Writers of the 20th Century*. Springfield, NJ: Enslow Publishers, 1996.

Brown, Jim. *Radar: How It All Began*. London: Janus, 1996.

Bryan, Jenny. *The History of Health and Medicine*. Austin, TX: Raintree/Steck-Vaughn, 1996.

Buchanan, A. Russell. *Black Americans in World War II*. Santa Barbara, CA: ABC-CLIO, 1977.

Burge, Michael C., and Don Nardo. *Vaccines: Preventing Disease*. San Diego, CA: Lucent Books, 1992.

Calvi, Gian. *How UNESCO Sees a World for Everybody*. Paris: UNESCO, 1979.

The Cambridge World History of Human Disease. New York: Cambridge University Press, 1993.

Camper, Erich. *Encyclopedia of the Olympic Games*. New York: McGraw-Hill, 1972.

Cayton, Andrew, Elizabeth I. Perry, and Allan M. Winkler. *America: Pathways to the Present: America in the Twentieth Century*. New York: Prentice Hall School Group, 1998.

Christopher, Matt. *Great Moments in Baseball History*. Boston: Little, Brown, 1996.

Chronicle of the Twentieth Century. Mount Cisco, NY: Chronicle, 1994.

Cohen, Daniel. *The Last 100 Years: Medicine*. New York: M. Evans, 1981.

Collier, Christopher. *Progressivism, the Great Depression, and the New Deal, 1901 to 1941*. New York: Benchmark Books/Marshall Cavendish, 2000.

Collier, Christopher, and James Lincoln Collier. *The United States in the Cold War*. New York: Benchmark Books/Marshall Cavendish, 2001.

Collins, Ace, and John Hillman. *Blackball Superstars: Legendary Players of the Negro Baseball Leagues*. Greensboro, NC: Avisson Press, 1999.

Companion Encyclopedia of the History of Medicine. London: Routledge, 1993.

Cook, Chris, and David Waller, eds. *The Longman Handbook of Modern American History, 1763–1996*. New York: Longman, 1998.

Cooper, Michael L. *Playing America's Game: The Story of Negro League Baseball*. New York: Lodestar Books, 1993.

Cozic, Charles P., ed. *Civil Liberties: Opposing Viewpoints*. San Diego, CA: Greenhaven Press, 1994.

Cunningham, Robert III, and Robert Cunningham Jr. *The Blues: A History of the Blue Cross and Blue Shield System*. DeKalb, IL: Northern Illinois University Press, 1997.

Decade of Triumph: The 40s. Alexandria, VA: Time-Life Books, 1999.

Diggins, John P. *The Proud Decades: America in War and in Peace, 1941–1960*. New York: Norton, 1988.

Donovan, Robert J. *The Second Victory: The Marshall Plan and the Postwar Revival of Europe*. New York: Madison Books, 1987.

Dorman, Michael. *Witch Hunt: The Underside of American Democracy*. New York: Delacorte Press, 1976.

Duden, Jane. *1940s*. New York: Crestwood House, 1989.

Dunnahoo, Terry Janson, and Herma Silverstein. *Baseball Hall of Fame*. New York: Maxwell Macmillan International, 1994.

Dunning, John. *Tune in Yesterday: The Ultimate Encyclopedia of Old-Time Radio 1925–1976*. Englewood Cliffs, NJ: Prentice-Hall, 1976.

Eaton, William Edward. *The American Federation of Teachers, 1916–1961: A History of the Movement*. Carbondale, IL: Southern Illinois University Press, 1975.

Encyclopedia of Technology and Applied Sciences. New York: Marshall Cavendish, 2000.

Engerman, Stanley L., and Robert E. Gallman, eds. *The Cambridge Economic History of the United States: The Twentieth Century (Vol 3)*. Cambridge: Cambridge University Press, 2000.

Faber, Doris, and Harold Faber. *American Literature*. New York: Atheneum Books for Young Readers, 1995.

Fariello, Griffin. *Red Scare: Memories of the American Inquisition, An Oral History*. New York: Norton, 1995.

Feinstein, Stephen. *The 1940s from World War II to Jackie Robinson*. Berkeley Heights, NJ: Enslow Publishers, 2000.

Foner, Eric, and John A. Garraty, eds. *The Reader's Companion to American History*. New York: Houghton Mifflin, 1991.

Freedman, Russell. *Martha Graham: A Dancer's Life*. New York: Clarion Books, 1998.

Garza, Hedda. *Women in Medicine*. New York: Franklin Watts, 1994.

Gordon, Karen. *Selman Waksman and the Discovery of Streptomycin*. Bear, DE: Mitchell Lane Publishers, 2002.

Gordon, Lois, et al. *American Chronicle: Year by Year through the Twentieth Century*. New Haven, CT: Yale University Press, 1999.

Goulart, Ron. *Comic Book Culture: An Illustrated History*. Portland, OR: Collector's Press, 2000.

Gould, William. *Boeing*. London: Cherrytree, 1995.

Gould, William. *Coca-Cola*. London: Cherrytree, 1995.

Where to Learn More

Grant, R.G. *Hiroshima and Nagasaki.* Austin, TX: Raintree/Steck-Vaughn, 1998.

Greenspan, Bud. *100 Greatest Moments in Olympic History.* Los Angeles: General Publishing Group, 1995.

Grimsley, Will. *Tennis: Its History, People, and Events.* Englewood Cliffs, NJ: Prentice Hall. 1971.

Gross, John, and the editors of *Golf Magazine. The Encyclopedia of Golf.* New York: Harper and Row, 1979.

Hall, Kermit L. *The Oxford Companion to the Supreme Court.* New York: Oxford University Press, 1992.

Harris, Cyril M. *American Architecture: An Illustrated Encyclopedia.* New York: W. W. Norton, 1998.

Hart, James David, and Philip Leininger, eds. *The Oxford Companion to American Literature.* New York: Oxford University Press, 1995.

Hatch, Shari Dorantes, and Michael R. Strickland, eds. *African-American Writers: A Dictionary.* Santa Barbara, CA: ABC-CLIO, 2000.

Heal, Edith. *The Teen-Age Manual: A Guide to Popularity and Success.* New York: Simon and Schuster, 1948.

Hills, Ken. *1940s.* Austin, TX: Raintree/Steck-Vaughn, 1992.

Hollander, Zander. *Home Run: Baseball's Greatest Hits and Hitters.* New York: Random House, 1984.

Hunt, Marsha. *The Way We Wore: Styles of the 1930s and '40s and Our World Since Then.* Fallbrook, CA: Fallbrook, 1993.

Isaacs, Sally Senzell. *America in the Time of Franklin Delano Roosevelt: The Story of Our Nation from Coast to Coast, from 1929 to 1948.* Des Plaines, IL: Heinemann Library, 2000.

Isaacs, Sally Senzell. *The Rise to World Power, 1929 to 1948.* Des Plaines, IL: Heinemann Library, 1999.

Italia, Bob. *100 Unforgettable Moments in Pro Tennis.* Edina, MN: Abdo & Daughters, 1996.

Jacobs, Jay. *The Color Encyclopedia of World Art.* New York: Crown Publishers, 1975

Janson, H. W. *History of Art.* New York: Abrams, 1995.

Jefferis, David. *Supersonic Flight.* New York: Franklin Watts, 1988.

Jones, Hettie. *Big Star Fallin' Mama: Five Women in Black Music.* New York: Viking, 1995.

Jordan, Matt Dukes. *Swankyville: A Guide to All That Swings.* Los Angeles: General Publishing Group, 1999

Kahn, Roger. *Games We Used to Play.* New York: Tickner and Fields, 1992.

Karl, Frederick R. *American Fictions, 1940–1980.* New York: Harper and Row, 1983.

Kevles, Daniel J. *The Physicists: The History of a Scientific Community in Modern America.* New York: Knopf, 1978.

Keylin, Arleen, and Jonathan Cohen, eds. *The Forties.* New York: Arno Press, 1980.

Landau, Elaine. *Tuberculosis.* New York: Franklin Watts, 1995.

Larsen, Rebecca. *Franklin D. Roosevelt: Man of Destiny.* New York: Franklin Watts, 1991.

Larson, Rebecca. *Oppenheimer and the Atomic Bomb.* New York: Franklin Watts, 1988.

Lee, Bruce, ed. *Roosevelt and Marshall: The War They Fought, the Change They Wrought.* New York: HarperTrade, 1991.

Lee, Winifred Trask. *A Forest of Pencils: The Story of Schools Through the Ages.* Indianapolis: Bobbs-Merrill, 1973.

Leonard, Thomas M. *Day by Day: The Forties.* New York: Facts on File, 1977.

Liss, Howard. *They Changed the Game: Football's Great Coaches, Players, and Games.* Philadelphia: Lippincott, 1975.

Lyons, Albert S. *Medicine: An Illustrated History.* New York: Abrams, 1978.

Manchel, Frank. *Women on the Hollywood Screen.* New York: Franklin Watts, 1977.

Margolick, David. *Strange Fruit: Billie Holiday, Cafe Society, and an Early Cry for Civil Rights.* Philadelphia: Running Press, 2000.

Martin, Richard. *Jocks and Nerds: Men's Style in the Twentieth Century.* New York: Rizzoli, 1989.

Matthews, Rupert. *Going to School.* New York: Franklin Watts, 2000.

May, Elaine Tyler. *Homeward Bound: American Families in the Cold War Era.* New York: Basic Books, 1988.

May, George S., ed. *Encyclopedia of American Business History and Biography: Banking and Finance, 1913–1989.* New York: Facts on File, 1990.

McCartney, Scott. *ENIAC: The Triumphs and Tragedies of the World's First Computer.* New York: Walker, 1999.

McCauley, Martin. *The Origins of the Cold War 1941–1949* New York: Addison Wesley, 1996.

McGilligan, Pat, ed. *Backstory 2: Interviews with Screenwriters of the 1940s and 1950s.* Berkeley: University of California Press, 1991.

McGrew, Roderick E. *Encyclopedia of Medical History.* New York: McGraw-Hill, 1985.

Melton, J. Gordon. *American Religions: An Illustrated History.* Santa Barbara, CA: ABC-CLIO, 2000.

Miller, Brandon Marie. *Just What the Doctor Ordered: The History of American Medicine.* Minneapolis: Lerner Publications, 1997.

Moloney, James H. *Encyclopedia of American Cars, 1930–1942.* Glen Ellyn, IL: Crestline, 1977.

Northrup, Mary. *American Computer Pioneers*. Springfield, NJ: Enslow Publishers, 1998.

Oermann, Robert K. *A Century of Country: An Illustrated History of Country Music*. New York: TV Books, 1999.

Olian, JoAnne. *Everyday Fashions of the Forties as Pictured in Sears Catalogs*. New York: Dover Publications, 1992.

O'Neal, Michael. *President Truman and the Atomic Bomb: Opposing Viewpoints*. San Diego, CA: Greenhaven Press, 1990.

Otfinoski, Steven. *Alexander Fleming: Conquering Disease with Penicillin*. New York: Facts on File, 1992.

Packard, Robert T., and Balthazar Korab. *Encyclopedia of American Architecture*. New York: McGraw-Hill, 1995.

Parker, Steve. *Medical Advances*. Austin, TX: Raintree/Steck-Vaughn, 1998.

Pease, Esther E. *Modern Dance*. Dubuque, IA: W. C. Brown Co., 1976.

Peper, George. *The Story of Golf*. New York: TV Books, 1999.

Porter, James A. *Modern Negro Art*. New York: Dryden Press, 1943.

Press, Petra. *A Multicultural Portrait of Learning in America*. New York: Marshall Cavendish, 1994.

Pulliam, John D. *History of Education in America*. Columbus, OH: Merrill, 1982.

Rabinowitz, Harold. *Classic Airplanes: Pioneering Aircraft and the Visionaries Who Built Them*. New York: MetroBooks, 1997.

Reef, Catherine. *Childhood in America*. New York: Facts on File, 2002.

Reynolds, Helen. *The 40s & 50s: Utility to New Look*. Milwaukee, WI: Gareth Stevens, 2000.

Robinson, Max, and Jack Kramer, eds. *The Encyclopedia of Tennis: One Hundred Years of Great Players and Events*. New York: Viking, 1974.

Rollin, Lucy. *Twentieth-Century Teen Culture by the Decades: A Reference Guide*. Greenwood Press. Westport, CT: 1999.

Royston, Angela. *100 Greatest Medical Discoveries*. Danbury, CT: Grolier Educational, 1997.

Ryan, Pat. *The Heavyweight Championship*. Mankato, MN: Creative Education, 1993.

Schatz, Thomas. *Boom and Bust: American Cinema in the 1940s*. Berkeley, CA: University of California Press, 1999.

Scheehan, Angela, ed. *The Marshall Cavendish Encyclopedia of Health*. New York: Marshall Cavendish, 1995.

Schraff, Anne E. *The Great Depression and the New Deal: America's Economic Collapse and Recovery*. New York: Franklin Watts, 1990.

Schuman, Michael A. *Harry S Truman*. New York: Enslow, 1997.

Seely, Bruce, ed. *Encyclopedia of American Business History and Biography: Iron and Steel in the Twentieth Century*. New York: Facts on File, 1993.

Seely, Gordon M. *Education and Opportunity: For What and For Whom?* Englewood Cliffs, NJ: Prentice-Hall, 1977.

Selden, Kyoko, and Mark Selden, eds. *The Atomic Bomb: Voices From Hiroshima and Nagasaki*. Armonk, NY: M. E. Sharpe, 1989.

Senior, Kathryn. *Medicine: Doctors, Demons, and Drugs*. New York: Franklin Watts, 1993.

Sherrow, Victoria. *Hiroshima*. New York: New Discovery Books, 1994.

Sicherman, Barbara, and Carol Hurd Green, eds. *Notable American Women: The Modern Period, a Biographical Dictionary*. Cambridge MA: Harvard University Press, 1980.

Sifakis, Carl. *The Encyclopedia of American Crime*. New York: Facts on File, 1982.

Silver, Alain, and Elizabeth Ward. *Film Noir: An Encyclopedic Reference to the American Style*. Woodstock, NY: Overlook Press, 1992.

Silverstein, Alvin, et al. *Polio*. Berkeley Heights, NJ: Enslow Publishers, 2001.

Simon, Charman. *Hollywood at War: The Motion Picture Industry and World War II*. New York: Franklin Watts, 1995.

Smith, Dian G. *Great American Film Directors: From the Flickers Through Hollywood's Golden Age*. New York: J. Messner, 1987.

Smith, Robert. *Illustrated History of Pro Football*. New York: Madison Square, 1970.

Snedden, Robert. *The History of Genetics*. New York: Thomson Learning, 1995.

Spiegelman, Art, and Chip Kidd. *Jack Cole and Plastic Man: Forms Stretched to Their Limits*. Mount Cisco, NY: Chronicle Books, 2001.

Spring, Joel. *The American School: 1642–1985*. New York: Longman, 1986.

Spring, Justin. *The Essential Jackson Pollock*. New York: Wonderland Press, Harry N. Abrams, 1998.

Stewart, Mark. *Baseball: A History of the National Pastime*. New York: Franklin Watts, 1998.

Stewart, Mark. *Basketball: A History of Hoops*. New York: Franklin Watts, 1998.

Stille, Darlene R. *Extraordinary Women of Medicine*. New York: Children's Press, 1997.

Stille, Darlene R. *Extraordinary Women Scientists*. Chicago: Children's Press, 1995.

Strubel, John Warthen. *The History of American Classical Music*. New York: Facts on File, 1995.

Stwertka, Albert, and Eve Stwertka. *Physics: From Newton to the Big Bang*. New York: Franklin Watts, 1986.

Taylor, Michael J. H., ed. *Jane's Encyclopedia of Aviation*. New York: Crescent Books, 1993.

Terkel, Studs. *The Good War: An Oral History of World War Two*. New York: Pantheon Books, 1984.

Terrace, Vincent. *The Complete Encyclopedia of Television Programs 1947–1979.* New York: Barnes, 1980.

Trotter, Joe William. *From a Raw Deal to a New Deal?: African Americans, 1929–1945.* New York: Oxford University Press, 1996.

Tucker, Sherrie. *Swing Shift: "All-Girl" Bands of the 1940s.* Durham, NC: Duke University Press, 2000.

Turner, Jane, ed. *The Dictionary of Art.* New York: Grove, 1996.

Uschan, Michael V. *Golf.* San Diego, CA: Lucent Books, 2001.

Uschan, Michael V. *The 1940s.* San Diego, CA: Lucent Books, 1999.

Wallenchinsky, David. *The Complete Book of the Olympics.* New York: Viking, 1984.

Whittingham, Richard. *Rites of Autumn: The Story of College Football.* New York: Free Press, 2001.

Wiedlich, Thom. *Appointment Denied: The Inquisition of Bertrand Russell.* Amherst, NY: Prometheus Books, 2000.

Wilds, Mary. *Raggin' the Blues: Legendary Country, Blues, and Ragtime Musicians.* Greensboro, NC: Avisson Press, 2001.

Willson, Quentin. *Classic American Cars.* New York: Dorling Kindersley, 1997.

Wind, Herbert Warren. *The Story of American Golf.* New York: Callaway Editions, 2000.

Wood, Tim, and R. J. Unstead. *The 1940s.* New York: Franklin Watts, 1990.

Yount, Lisa. *Genetics and Genetic Engineering.* New York: Facts on File, 1997.

Yount, Lisa. *History of Medicine.* San Diego, CA: Lucent Books, 2001.

PERIODICALS

"The 101 Great Ideas." *Life* (January 26, 1948): pp. 92-102.

WEB SITES

Ad Access: Brief History of World War Two Advertising Campaigns. [Online] http://scriptorium.lib.duke.edu/adaccess/wwad-history.html (accessed March 2002).

America from the Great Depression to World War II: Photographs from the FSA-OWI, 1935–1945. [Online] http://memory.loc.gov/ammem/fsahtml/fahome.html (accessed March 2002).

American Institute of Physics: Center For History of Physics. [Online] http://www.aip.org/history/ (accessed August 2002).

American Red Cross History: 1940–1959. [Online] http://www.redcross.org/museum/19401959.html (accessed March 2002).

Blue Cross and Blue Shield History. [Online] http://www.bcbs.com/whoweare/history.html (accessed March 2002).

College Football Hall of Fame. [Online] http://www.collegefootball.org/ (accessed February 2002).

Cyber Boxing Zone. [Online] http://cyberboxingzone.com/ (accessed April 2002).

FDR Library and Digital Archives: K12 Learning Center. [Online] http://www.fdr-library.marist.edu/teach.html (accessed March 2002).

George C. Marshall Foundation. [Online] http://www.marshallfoundation.org/about_gcm/marshall_plan.htm (accessed March 2002).

Great Buildings Online. [Online] http://www.greatbuildings.com (accessed March 2002).

Hales, Peter Bacon. Levittown: Documents of an Ideal American Suburb. [Online] http://tigger.uic.edu/~pbhales/Levittown.html (accessed March 2002).

The History of Education and Childhood. [Online] http://www.socsci.kun.nl/ped/whp/histeduc/index.html (accessed March 2002).

Major League Baseball History. [Online] http://mlb.mlb.com/NASApp/mlb/mlb/history/mlb_history_awards.jsp (accessed April 2002).

NASA X-1 Fiftieth Anniversary Homepage. [Online] http://www.hq.nasa.gov/office/pao/History/x1/index.html (accessed August 2002).

National Archives and Records Administration. Powers of Persuasion: Poster Art from World War II. [Online] http://www.nara.gov/exhall/powers/powers.html (accessed March 2002).

National Baseball Hall of Fame. [Online] http://www.baseballhalloffame.org/ (accessed April 2002).

National Records and Archives Administration: The Marshall Plan. [Online] http://www.nara.gov/exhall/featured-document/marshall/marshall.html (accessed March 2002).

Pro Football Hall of Fame. [Online] http://www.profootballhof.com/ (accessed April 2002).

Spruce Goose Exhibition. [Online] http://www.aero.com/museums/evergreen/evergrn.htm (accessed March 2002).

St. John's College: Where Great Books Are the Teachers. [Online] http://www.sjca.edu (accessed March 2002).

Truman Presidential Museum and Library. [Online] http://www.trumanlibrary.org/index.html (accessed March 2002).

Women in Baseball: All-American Girls' Professional Baseball League. [Online] http://www.acusd.edu/%7Ejsartan/AAGBL.htm (accessed April 2002).

Index